BOOMER BYTES & BUMMER RITES

NEERJA SINGH

INDIA • SINGAPORE • MALAYSIA

ISBN 978-1-68494-673-0

Dedication

For my girl Aqseer, her courageous life and fearless living

Do you hear me Aqs?

If only I had known our moment that day would be our last

Contents

Preface

The 7th Dec 2021.

Aqseer, with a 'q', my 31-year-old self-driven, highly accomplished and insanely talented millennial daughter called it a wrap on earth and declared, "I am all done here!" She was barely two months away from turning 32. Her father and I had gone to the Roshni Counselling Centre at Hyderabad, 3.8 km from our home, to keep our appointment with the psychologist at 12.30 noon, when my phone pinged. It was our domestic, "Didi has been in the washroom too long!"

Her last conversation was with me on the terrace of our home, about 10.45 am that morning. Ironically, it was one-sided. I spoke and she listened. I made a statement, "Aqseer, even a person with depression is responsible for getting well." There was a pause. Then she got up with a resolve, picked up the two mugs of chai we had emptied and walked down the steps to her room…to take charge. That was it.

Ironic because Aqseer's professional life as a law graduate and a therapist had all been about one thing, "Shut up and listen!" All her start-up merchandizes carried this message. She advocated listening skills for wellness. Shut up and listen! It came from her belief that radical differences in generational preferences, priorities and prejudices had become tangible issues today. She and I often spoke of how generational diversity could be both a headache and a help depending on whether or not we shut up and listened to each other.

I believe Aqseer's case is representative of the fragile and volatile ecosphere our educated, urban, upper middle-class youth grapple with today. They struggle to establish themselves in a traumatized global order while fighting the inertia of tradition.

And I am not alone in this devil's advocacy. According to the World Health Organization, youth suicide is an emerging and serious public health issue in India. In 2019, the age groups of 18–30 and 30–45 years accounted for 67% of total suicides. And it keeps rising.

Our young are marching to unfamiliar tunes. For instance, all the check boxes ticked for Aqseer. An ivy league education, supportive family, good looks and talent…no dearth of skills or teachers and coaches and gurus but we kept hearing, "All I need is a mentor, someone to hold my hand and show me how to be and feel enough," and that did not happen.

The exposure my generation valued is drowning the young with its unfiltered waterfall of information today. In addition to her education in the law and psychology and the inevitable side-effects of medicines, the resistance to treatment that we faced from our daughter came from her extensive reading online about the big pharma frauds.

The Internet's extra-constitutional influence does not factor in socio-cultural coordinates. New Age Platforms, peers, online gurus and special friends have greater access to and currency with our young than parents. No one knows for sure, what influences are shaping them. We have all bought into the popular script that they are smarter and so long as they are happy, it is all good. But smartness is not retrospective wisdom and happiness is ephemeral…it has to be earned every moment. But who will spell this out? My generation has lost the courage to risk unpopularity with our young, we fear estrangement from them, we are wary of playing the paternal card.

The good news is that while young people are both likely to have greater behavioural health issues, they are also more willing to talk openly about psychological well-being and to seek assistance. Aqseer founded a mental health initiative of her own called Aaina Therapy. Her point was that the "don't ask, don't tell" approach to mental health at home and in the workplace has to become "do ask, do tell" and then "let's talk."

The real work involved however is of social and culture change. It did not help my daughter's recovery to have the therapist, family, psychiatrist and friends work in silos. Generational competence mandates support of the entire village in a spirit of benevolence and openness. Just as Aqseer needed a middle ground that brought together psychology, medicine and spirituality to address her horrific struggle, generational thrival will come from a culture of care, better communication practices and an evolved sense of empathy.

Aqseer needed a wellness program that went beyond diet and exercise to include financial well-being and mental health. She needed help and tools she could relate to. What she needed was a partner in health, not an expert or an authority figure.

Have you been affected by the generational gap in attitude, knowledge and skills? Would you agree it is time for kindness and over-communication? Aqseer needed psychological safety. She was crying for flexibility, establishing boundaries, and creating new norms around connections.

I made mistakes. I took things personally. I took time to get a generational education and then to embrace the differences. I could have shut up and listened more with a keener empathy. I should have ennobled talk of overcoming behavioural health challenges. I could have appreciated better Aqseer's looming loneliness. I could have helped make navigation of the system easier for her.

Some questions will remain forever. Was it a simple case of a genetic predisposition getting triggered by stressful life events such as the boy who spoke commitment and then began ghosting her? Did she receive the support a more evolved ecosystem could have given her? What toll did generational grief take on her fight to be truly herself, independent of anyone's approval?

Aqseer lit many fires down here, she raged and loved and howled and laughed and fought with every fibre of her being. She forced us, her family, to open up our hearts and minds and souls. Like a tornado, she swept us along, magnificent in her empathy for others and the courage of her convictions. But it was uphill to speak up for those without voices, it was exhausting to keep sane society at bay, it broke her heart to feel alone at the end of an eventful, impactful but tumultuous life.

She gave the world Peer Support Groups, Delhi High Court Hearing on Mental Health on College Campuses, Protective Nets in Nizamuddin, PsychPros, Blacksheep Unite, Transgender Rights, Kink Affirmative Therapy, Queer Feminism…she claimed her space, she fought for Public Conveniences for Women, she sat in on the Citizenship Amendment Act, Slutwalk Bangalore…her brand Aaina Therapy…she said she felt the safest driving her Alto on the roads of Delhi at 2 am in the night, giving us the jitters. She badly wanted a partner. I did not think her match existed in this world.

Aqseer had wanted to get married in a green and red Masaba Gupta designer saree. My mother bought it and readied it for her despite my protests. Aqseer did wear the drape and the smartly tailored blouse on her final journey to the crematorium. Her sister made her up with a bindi and lipstick and flowers in the hair.

Aqseer, with a 'q', lived and left on her own terms. But the generations need to come together and co-create cumulative, compassionate and collaborative terms. This onus is collective.

The stakes are sky high, there is only but to listen or die.

My millennial (born 1981 to 1996) is gone but this book is an account for her, of the follies of life from her boomer's (born 1946 to 1964) lens.

Neerja Singh

Aqseer's Proud Mother

neerja@neerjasingh.com

I

IN REVERIE

1
The Walk

Have you ever walked in the rain? On a track in a park adjoining the road. The falling water merges with the traffic buzz. The smoky sky turns turgid, and you reach for the phone. There is a fellow feeling in the wet air, a by-product of the isolation rain causes. The footsteps squelch, and the napkin gives up. The genetic beauty in the flower beds begins to quiver in delight. The streak of water, forming a trombone, gathers speed on the wide-palm leaves. Rocks glisten. Dogs shake their ears. Lovers draw closer. A busy mother breaks her quick stride to bow to the Hanuman temple across the road. Walkers file hurriedly towards the asbestos awning. A solo young man lifts his face to the scattered spray, his back pressing into the trunk. The light begins to fade, and you quicken towards the car park, hugging to yourself thoughts of tangy hot soup! But the car splutters, the engine coughs, and you turn frantic, playing the key and working your toe on the throttle. Rain is coming down in opaque sheets now, and the windows are beginning to fog up. You slide down in your driving seat in misery. Home seems a long way off. You hate to bother your family to haul themselves out in this weather for you, but your adrenal is squirting now; your stomach heaves at the thought of Nirbhaya and Priyanka Reddy. You remind yourself that you are in your own country where you pay taxes and that you have not committed a crime by choosing to step out for a walk in this weather. But you are a woman, and this is no country for one.

2

The Rebel

Have you noticed the rigid boredom? On faces and in eyes, living everyday life. The minds running ahead of words. You are there yet far away. Someone is directing words at you; their mouth is opening and closing. You are nodding and shaking your head too, but you have checked out. There are, after all, appointments to keep, the gym to log, at least twenty-three tasks howling for deliverance. But not to worry, there are pretty words to do the masking and maintain a pretence of civility. Try these. "Awesome!" "Excellent!" "Out of this world!" The air we breathe swarms with adulterated anaesthesia, a numb flakiness. There is no break anywhere for a genuine emotion; the idea is to get on with it. But then, just as your brain begins to resign itself to all the white noise around, out pops a face… eyes glittering, breath rasping, energy barely reigned in. That body is clearly straining upstream, the need for personal affirmation straining under the courteous smile. Your antenna locks on to that curiously beautiful obstinacy around the germ of a fertile idea. You recognize their courage to challenge the comfort and ease of the status quo. Someone else is thrashing too! They are reaching out and beyond the prescribed. It proves we are indeed born to expand in our consciousness. And sure, the dream begins to stir! Never mind that the family is waiting to tell you how it all must be thought through thoroughly and that there are all these pitfalls ahead and better know that it has never been done before. How utterly remarkable that enterprises such as Zomato and CommonFloor.com and Aaina Therapy have come up. Despite the Indian family.

3

The Leader

Have you felt betrayed? The taste is particularly acrid when the powerful fail to assert their authority in your favour. *It is a sell-out,* you tell yourself. Our leaders have feet of clay. Those in positions of privilege must carry the world on their shoulders. Their oversight is the cause of our shabby environs. If they had bite, we would live well-oiled lives. You know all about how power goes to the head, and then it becomes about making sure that their personal boats stay afloat forever. It is a great line to take for self-preservation. If the leaders lack courage, what good is a small fry? It relieves you of your responsibility. "Our tigers have become so tame today that anyone can pull their tail and run." But take a look around; many of yours are probably counting on you to play the leader in your personal and professional solar system. You have more power than you think. Perhaps you have not spoken up enough. Have you challenged archaic perceptions ever? How often did you take refuge in silence when mischief was brewing in plain sight? Do you follow the convenient philosophy of "personal is not political"? It is entirely feasible that you have had no incentive to change. A numb and blasé acceptance; even indifference has set in. Just like your leaders. But more than ever before, today is the time to show up. And on the side of affirmative and assertive gentleness. The era of me and mine is coming to a close. The world is too flat for that brand of self-seeking.

4

The Game

Which side of golf are you on? Maybe it leaves you cold, even irritated at the time, with an apparent lack of skill involved. The voice in your head probably marvels at the doddering bunch of fogeys shuffling after a silly marble. Pretentious brown sahibs, you chuckle to yourself, dabbing clean skin with cool white towels. It seems almost criminal—the man-hours involved. And what about the resources needed to keep a course going? But there indeed are, in that inheritance from the Raj, moments of magic. There is sweet solitude in walking the damp grass to the next shot in moderate companionship. Nothing to beat the frissons of daybreak air brushing the limbs as you aim and swing. The birds trill. An eagle swoops down at a tasty twig to glide away with power. Your eye comes to rest on a stray plastic bit being teased by the breeze. Cries of anguish and ecstasy ring at birdies hit and the pars invariably missed! A moist garnish of dust glimmers in the distance, winking at the delusion of control littering the fairway. Men and women wage private battles of stamina and spirit in public. It takes courage to get out there, be under the constant glare of the invariably judgmental caddies! Every night you set the alarm and go to bed, visualizing that perfect follow through. But they await you, the merciless draws and fades and the shanks and punches, and yet you persevere, moving up, a shot at a time. Then, on a rare day, the Hand of God happens. And you keep coming back!

5

The Gate

Have you come out of the wrong gate of a public park at nightfall ever? The resultant disorientation stops you in the tracks, and a quick sense of alarm stabs at the heart; your neck swivels in confusion. The last few vehicles are pulling out of the parking, and the homebound traffic is frantic. You shut your eyes, mustering images of familiar landmarks, in an attempt to start back home. But it is inevitable; you will take the wrong turn in an onrush of anxiety. You will advance along the unfamiliar lane rapidly, despite the faint trepidation, casting about for human directions only to be told to take a U-turn now. "How far? How much further?" It is quite usual to scan the recommended distance in disbelief. "How could you have missed the exit? It all looks so different in the dark!" You begin to beat yourself up a bit. An autorickshaw slows down on the deserted road only to spur you on towards a homeless huddle. Thank heaven for a PCR Van. You are perversely glad at the timing of the traffic challan party; there is still some distance to go, and it is reassuring to have company, even though a confrontational one. The glare of the hurtling traffic calls for coordination and focus, and just as you are swinging indecisively on the ball of your foot, it comes into view: the familiar hotel, your lifeline of a marker. The muscles ease up, and you exhale with relief, cruising home with confidence now. But what's this here? No one seems to have missed you!

6

The Survivor

Have you tested your comfort level ever? Why would you when you have spent a lifetime attaining certainty and security? It all looks like it is in place finally. Well, not everything but most of it. A beautiful house, children settled into decent jobs, who are perhaps taking too long to marry or have kids, but your pension is assured, and you are not dependent on them, God forbid. It is a regular, neat, and predictable world. There is that support from the immediate family, the functional workplace where you have made some kind of a mark, and a couple of golden, evergreen childhood friendships. You have a sure sense of self, of your place in the scheme of things, and a life view nearly set in stone. Then along comes a pebble, plop! in this personal placid lake of yours. Life brings surprises, rude ones at times. You are forced to step out of your picture-book world. You meet people you would ordinarily never encounter. There are visits to places you did not consider your type. You scramble on strange roads, pinching yourself. Could you have anticipated it all? Should you have done things differently? Is the worst over? You grow cross-eyed at the heartbreaking harshness of it all. You come close to throwing in the towel, but instead, you decide to hunker down. One tentative step after another, one improvised decision after another, one confrontation after another…a muscle and sinew at a time, heart in the mouth, your spirit sore with all the beating. You begin to slowly raise yourself. It is in the nature of life. It's a fight, this business of living!

7

The Zone

Have you been in the zone ever? It is akin to a state of meditation. The world recedes, a cocoon of intense concentration envelops you, the sense of the moment is heightened, and the light is sharper. You could be painting, composing music, writing, or simply cooking. It is just the two of you…the self and that task consuming you. There is an alignment of desire and outcome, a silver amalgam of talent and opportunity. You don't hear someone calling; you chafe at interruptions. Oh, how you want the world to be still. You are creating! You are putting together something new that is uniquely you. There you go, digging deep into the innards of your being to draw out a complex stream of thoughts, emotions, and impressions. Was this raw material lying in your head all this while? Or did you pluck it from the air? What levers did you push to synchronize your faculties into that one melting melody, that life-like portrait, that bestseller of a book, that breath-taking finish at the ribbon, that gutsy adventure, that defiant flight, that stubborn come back? How does science explain inspired actions? Or emotional drive? Where is man's original stock of humanity? What are we constantly reflecting in our push to be at peace? Those calls for just being, that state of merely existing, devoid of quest or hunger—does that not call for extreme ambition and ego? Should every man and woman acquire detachment? How much lesser would human existence be without our anguished creations, those cries from our souls for validation, for acknowledgment, for our desire to be done on earth in a clean, complete, compelling way! Whose manifestations are we, after all?

8

The Boutique

Have you entered a boutique store that is way beyond your reach and that you have no intentions of patronizing? Let's just take a look, you have told yourself. You merely want to check out the current sartorial trends. The floor knows it; the salespeople can tell with one look what a waste of their time you are going to be, but everyone gets on with the act. You smile grimly, deliberately casual as you riffle through the expensive garments. "What's the fabric?" you ask with an air of nonchalance, craning your neck towards the price tag all the time. You hold the vain off-shoulder gown up and away, laying it over your frame, going so far as to look around for a mirror, then swivelling besides a friend before placing it back with finality. "Thank you!" your smile turns saccharine, "Let me come back again. I'll just go around a bit." The salesperson's smirk fades; she has heard this before. She watches you make your escape. A sign on the shop door catches your eye: "Asking for discounts embarrasses us." The two of you chuckle delicately and advance towards the next designer store and their hapless salesperson. Another visiting card gets shoved into the peculiar handbags, one more technical talk on where the lovely creations have come from and how fast the colours are and whether they can be machine washed, and you pull away politely to execute as unobtrusive an exit as you can. You lumber past swinging bags with designer labels hung on chic shoulders. One of you erupts, "My goodness, where do these people get all that money from? It must be black!"

9

The Exclusive

Have you been embarrassed turning up at a party in a saree someone else happens to be draped in too? Identical colour and similar fabric. And, heaven help you both, the border matches too. Good Lord! The event leaves a mark. You try to make light of it, laughing it off, even inviting the other lady to play hostess at the gate. "Let's form a reception committee!" But it rankles; the social euphoria dims, and you feel lesser. Not your fault. No, it isn't. We have been sold exclusivity to the nth degree! Times were when siblings happily wore frocks and bushirts cut from the same bolt of fabric. The lace, the piping, the bows down to the organdie roses, the replications were faithful, and nobody gave it a second thought. There was an unspoken kinship of sameness, a sense of belonging to a tribe. No one dreamt of associating similarity with a deeply personal sense of loss. Truth be told, those were monochromatic times. Between the Ambassador and Fiat, Hamam and Lifebuoy, Binaca and Colgate, Ponds and Nivea…there was only so much distinction. The modern gluttony of choices was still some decades away. The appearance had not yet become the classist issue it is today. Exclusivity did not play as great a role in everybody's sense of self-worth. "Hatke" was not a religion yet. We have come a long way since. Friends and family would frequently cross-check the odd, commonly owned accessory they are wearing to a function now, just in case. No one wants to deal with the shame of being common. Funny we should all want the same thing when all we want is to appear different!

10

The Forward

Have you ever deleted several WhatsApp forwards without reading them and from dear friends you would ordinarily launch gushing at with outstretched arms and half a dozen muah muahas? You bet there is a setting you have tweaked right so that the graphics-heavy files do not obliterate your phone memory with their tsunami of colour and content. You have the drill on auto by now: flip open the phone, scroll hurriedly down the green ticks, peer at the translucent squares with their cheery heralding of the morning—fortunately, the "Good afternoon" and "Good evening", and "Good night" greetings have not caught on yet—then select delete. You slap the phone down, wipe a trickle of sweat, and lean your throbbing head back. Such invasion of the senses! There are the videos to be dealt with yet! Most informative and entertaining, many of them, but investment heavy in terms of time and digital currency. And the groups! Alma maters, colony, block, meetups, satsang, craft artists, dog lovers, family old and family young, the sisters-in-law, kitty meet, religion-based, childhood friends, groups within groups…oh, you dare not leave those. You half perch there, shifting weight from one aching foot to another. You try hard. You really do. You are, after all, the recipient of several blessed weekdays and peaceful weekend wishes. With a festival every day in India, including Bhishma Ashtami and Paush Purnima, your incoming WhatsApp notification beeps a three-digit figure in no time. So much deleting homework! Just as you have freed up your mobile, along comes a surprisingly short one. It says GM/GN. But then there follows an extended polka-dotted pattern. You stare at it, fighting your wickedness!

11

The Collapse

Have you felt lately your kids value opinion of their same-age peers more than they value yours? Your parental authority has declined; their natural dependence on you has shifted to their contemporaries, but hey, you are a modern parent even though a thoroughly confused one. Moreover, who is going to risk alienation with a generation that has access to social families outside of their parental homes? You've also mistaken the new generation's digital nativity for life smarts. "Let's be their friend! Let's not crowd them with our inputs and feedback. They are global citizens, and the world is their oyster!" The carpet is all set now; it starts to be pulled out from under you. You run faster, arms flailing in the air… Darn! Where is that kid with his shoulder? What happened to the glow of gratitude? You smell dismissive contempt; an accusation or two even. "Get a life folks! Back off! Chill! Seek therapy, please. I can't do this anymore. Give me my space!" Even the schools have begun to fight shy of teaching any absolute notions of good behaviour. They have instead taken to suggesting that a child has ADHD or Hyperactivity or Oppositional Defiant Disorder. There is no Bill of Rights, after all, for teachers or parents. The cult of youth, a culture of disrespect and declining social skills…more and more children are bringing up each other. Their top priority is pleasing their friends and finding acceptance with them. Parents are rapidly becoming, well, almost an afterthought, a post script, a portal for laundry/finance/ laptop management. But, of course, this is not true of you and me, just the rest of the world, the United States of America, in particular!

12

The Comparison

Have you cast surreptitious looks at your neighbour's order while the waiter is placing your selection in front of you? No matter how much you apply yourself to selecting from the varied choices from the menu, that dish sailing right past your table looks more appetizing than the platter in front of you. Chances are you have beckoned the service boy closer and asked him in low tones, pointing in that particular direction of interest with a quick stab of the chin, "What are they eating?" Not your fault. Nature has made us like that. Insecure and covetous and envious to the core. All for the sake of human survival but of course. Why, it is not enough to just listen to someone's story of glory and leave it with a polite expression of admiration! You have to juxtapose it against your own experience so as to make it somewhat palatable. A friend shares news of his adventure trip, and you launch into how your backache has restrained you from going on similar expeditions. The neighbour drops by with sweets, celebrating their new car, and you go getting into the nitty gritty of your own transport fleet comprising all of two beat up Maruti vans. Someone's got themselves a nice haircut, and we simply must pat our pates, deliberating haircare resources. Ever seen someone dance well? You feel compelled to explain away your two left feet. There is a flip side though to this theme of begrudging. Mere admiration would have been passive. Envy, on the other hand, could well be motivating!

13

The Acquaintance

Have you ever gotten stuck walking a loop in the park an acquaintance is pounding too? And from the opposite direction. Now you are meeting over and over! The first time you come face to face, there is abundant warmth, an extravagant invite to home even. You both part smiling. *Must remember to mention this to family*, you think idly, gathering self-congratulatory pace. But guess what? He is nearly upon you again, and there's been no space to compose your face. The first-time effervescence is clearly out, but ignoring altogether would be equally inappropriate. You settle on a semi-grin that says, "I like you, but we just met!" You both hurry past each other purposefully. Now the radars begin to scan in preparation for the third encounter. Some twenty feet of each other, you fix your gaze on the pathway, in a trance over gravel. But, lo and behold, your mental antennas are convulsing, your thoughts lock on, and your bowed heads snap up in unison. There is a sheepish "Hello again!" *This can't go on*, you tell yourself. You don't know each other well enough to stride along, and you are not strangers enough for the closed look. You decide to get original. You pick strategic bushes to duck into. There is an inner ring you identify for a quick side stepping. "*This might be the time to try even the public toilet*," you tell yourself. In that split break of the social fuel, your limbs take over and your frame does a clumsy about-turn. You bump into a body. Your acquaintance has had the exact same idea!

14

The Invite

Have you ever invited someone, knowing fully well they will not attend? Congratulations! You killed two birds with one stone. You got brownie points for graciousness, and you engineered some thrifty resource management at the same time. What are the facts as you know them to be true? Your innocent invitees are perhaps embroiled in an irksome family event. They could be hiking around the unbearably scenic Croatian countryside. They may have shared details of an ongoing illness with you at some point in your association. There is no way they will be able to make it—you are two hundred percent certain of that. But you go right ahead and extend a formal invite anyway. You have done your bit! Now they are free to send across a gift or just ignore the gesture. They cannot feel bad about being left out. They might even have wanted a keepsake of the event they will miss. This way they have the flexibility should there be a change in their status. You have thought this through. You almost begin to bask in delusions of your personal magnanimity and walk in, all glowing, to the coordination committee meet. There is so much to tie up. The catering, the décor, the transport, the local itinerary, the rooms allocation, the entertainment, and most of all the budget! At the end of all the heavy duty ticking on and slashing off the "To-do" list, someone starts to take a dread-filled final count of the invitees. The figures on the calculator are swelling up. Hearts begin to beat. On cue, you jump up gleefully and announce to the host committee reassuringly, "Those ones are not coming!"

15

The Winnow

Have you ever had someone standing close by tidy you up in a social setting? Someone ever advance at your eyes to dab at a kohl smudge? A lightening tug maybe at the saree *pallu* so it aligns better. You have had a dry cleaner's label pointed out with the broadest half-smile. And heaven help you if you have spent the morning strutting in pants screaming "499/-" on the back of the thigh. Oh, yes, it is entirely within the realm of possibility to take that confident step out, wearing a garment inside out or back to front. And who has not arrived at parties wearing the wrong shade of a dark coloured bindi? It is telling though, what follows. There is a conspiratorial air to the straightening, a furtive edge to the plucking, and almost a sense of shame at having a speck tweezed off your jacket. Your face falls into a flat smile, only the corners turning up while your well-wishers move in, shielding you from the imaginary curious eyes. That pesky garment, moreover, which makes a ritual of playing peek-a-boo, elicits a more elaborate social charade. Smug as a sacred cow, your friend closes in, pretend gazing in the wrong direction. She sticks her two fingers along the shoulder and under the fabric only to stuff the offending strap out of sight. You go a bit red in the face, still trying to make up your mind whether to kick yourself at all when you catch sight of a person coming at you oozing childhood warmth, hands outstretched in melodramatic nostalgia. You crumble on the sofa, a sitting duck. What is the faux pas now?

16

The Eyes

Have you ever broken eye contact in a hurry? Abruptly even. It felt too close for comfort. There was a vast, silent, living presence there… witnessing, accepting, fighting at times and then patiently waiting out this lifetime of the owner. It is one of the most powerfully intimate of human experiences. Just looking into each other's eyes, be they friends, family, strangers, or your partner. Eyes incredibly are your soul's Google Pay. Those gel orbs with their patterned flecks hold folders on living, breathing moments of pleasure and pain, sadness and joy, expectations and disappointments. Some entity there seems to keep an eternal tally. There was that time you hovered over a tight circle at a party and no one made way to let you in. You made several announcements of your impending departure from home but no family member stopped long enough to wave a white handkerchief. There was this one time you offered your hand for an eager shake but the target walked off, leaving your hand limp in mid-air. And remember that lady whose eyes kept scanning the peopled lawn whilst you were narrating a moving personal incident to her. Life lurches along and bygones do become bygones. But your eyes. Oh! your eyes have it all. They retain and reflect your crying need for acknowledgement. Your desire to do your parents proud. Your abiding need to see your children flourish. Your fumbling attempts at establishing a mutually fulfilling intimacy with your partner. Your anguish at a pet's suffering. Your fear of uncertainty. Your strife. Your self-doubt. Your stubborn spirit. Eyes are never quiet! Until the end, that is.

17

The Freeze

Have you ever been consistently given a cold dismissal by someone? Persistently! Without a break. It is arctic, the icicles tickling the nook of your elbows and the dimples in your knees. You put up a valiant fight to find acceptance with them. Cracking grins and forward bends, eager to please tips of the head. Nada! You continue to shiver and languish in the chill of their rejection. Like the carcasses, you have been confined to their deep freeze. Why? What did you do to them? Could a mutual acquaintance have shared an uncomplimentary anecdote you regaled them with in one of your reckless moods? It is entirely possible you were abrupt with them at some point in time. Unknowingly! Maybe they don't consider you enough of a nuisance to be bothered with. But there is a connection, even though a testy one. You sense it. The blue chill is palpable. They know you exist. Their eyes bounce off your body often enough, never really connecting. Their malevolence, like a body bag, zipping you in, wholly and darkly. You tango often to come into their view, but they look through you, past you, above you, beyond you. There are flashes of hope at a covert glance or two, but those again die down with stony shivers. You are numb now, hallucinating that it is in fact indifference that you have mistaken for rejection. "*Why should I care?*" you tell yourself, ready to cut the cord when a friend cosies up, "Listen! Mrs. Kumar feels you give her the cold shoulder. She finds you downright icy. What's up with you? You need to take a chill pill, friend!"

18

The Monument

Have you lived in Agra twenty years and not seen the Taj Mahal? Were you born in Allahabad but never visited the Anand Bhavan? Spent seven years in Jhansi without ever setting a foot inside the Rani Mahal. Been home to Benares annually with no clue as to the existence of Pehalwan ki Lassi. "*I have plenty of time! I am not going anywhere,*" you have told yourself. You know in principle that you are mortal, but you have envisioned that conclusive event a long way off in your head. With your illusory logic, you have defined the limits of your personal experience, and you are too busy now to challenge those. There you go, all frazzled and abuzz, keeping your appointments with your three meals a day. There is the afternoon siesta, phone calls to the kids, chaat masala to grind, dental and mental upkeep. Who has the time to venture behind structures and monuments or institutions? You'd be surprised at their inner dynamic were you to step into one. They are the why and the how of the towns and cities we inhabit. Knowing about the men and women behind them, their motivations and consciences, their struggles and strife…who knows how it might shift our perspective! We could in fact be the links in the survival of our culture. When we go gorging on sights and the ice creams, we are in fact helping preserve our heritage! Care to spare a thought for the minds and hearts behind our surroundings the next time we stop to arrange ourselves for that monumental selfie?

19

The Ride

Have you ever looked on at someone advertising their century bicycle ride with the thought, "*Wow! I'd like to do that too. What fun the group seems to be having! And such happy pictures! What am I doing, sitting here?*" You are not to be blamed for this self-flogging. The impression you are going by is only half the story. In those vibrant frames on Facebook, where are the sore buttocks and the fiery toes? Is there any mention of the steam engine breaths and empty lungs? The sun drinks your sap up in greedy gulps on those rides. Barring the odd pit stop, you dare not fall behind. The ride has to be completed. It is your pact with yourself. Moreover, your family is sitting inside your head; you will not go back to them with a pull out. You pedal, therefore, despite the cramps and the dry mouth. There are tricks you use to keep your resolve robust. On those dreaded slopes, you fix your gaze three feet beyond the front wheel. You concentrate on the gear combinations; even a glance at the painfully long curve ahead could cause the spirits to flag. There is a thin, a very thin line in the mind that separates persistence from surrender. Don't be alarmed at the queasy stomach. Hydrate yourself! That shoulder on fire is from the shocking bumps in the road. Keep moving, one pedal at a time. Bite into some chocolate or roll a candy around in the mouth. You will see the ice cream carts and crave the lick lollies. The sight of Limca bottles behind a vendor will drive you crazy with lust. You will suffer a flat tyre. Your Allen key will bounce out of the stem pouch to shatter on the expressway. But you will stay in the saddle. Hours will go by; every muscle, every sinew crying for you to stop, but you will labour on, chafed and throbbing on the machine. The reward? That blooming voice in the head telling you, "You did it!"

20

The Call

Have you surpassed all Oscar winning performances in the radius of your mobile phone? Say it vibrates in the middle of a conversation; you steal a quick glance and dip the silencer if it is the mum-in-law. For mum, the default setting is an apologetic smile and a rapid getaway. The response protocol is in place, all of it. You keep your ringer turned on in public spaces, taking calls just to inform the caller grandly that you are in a movie hall and will call once home. Should the boss be calling, you sit through six rings while you gauge and rack your brains as to what the call could be about. Your precious progeny is not responding? You promptly sneak into WhatsApp to confirm when they were last online, out of concern. Oh, you are smart! Strange, unfamiliar numbers do not have the power to trap you ordinarily. But what if you have won a freebie or a TV offer? What if your child is calling from a stranger's phone for help? You call back the number cautiously at such moments of self-doubt but then disconnect promptly, beeping at the automated "Priya grahak." You observe all the rules: carry the phone to the loo, continue to scream into it even when there is no network, not let up on Candy crush, scroll FB and twitter updates while on landline, use driving time to make calls. And who hasn't told lies to cover for a family member who does not want to come to the phone? Many of us ourselves have found precisely that moment to disappear into the washroom or be out on a supposed walk. While life hurries to happen to us only when the phone is charging, watch us Ninjafy should someone so much as touch our doodah!

21

The Facial

Have you ever felt your abject need for beauty treatment rubbed into your face at the salon you happened to be patronizing? They rain questions on you. "When did you last trim your hair, madam? How long since you had your nose plucked free of black spots? Have you not oiled your hair ever? Has your skin always been this dry? We have this excellent Vampire facial that will take away ten years from your face!" While you squirm and cringe at this barrage, the attendant takes on the persona of a crisis manager who is about to begin to build you from scratch. A strange hand with painted talons lifts a lock of your hair, almost with distaste. Another pair makes a grab for your feet, muttering under their breath. "Cuticles are not all that bad!" A third begins to thread away with forceful swipes, blaming the colour of your eyebrows for the eventual outcome. And my condolences over the inflamed temples as your colourist goes at dabs of leftover dye with gusto. Take heart! No one looks anything like their rear-view image the day after the blow drying of the hair. You are finally done! The air stings your newly scrubbed, waxed, threaded skin. You feel lighter at the least. The heels are baby smooth yet; curls and waves sitting pretty on your shoulders. It is time to settle. The document is drawn up, the service hands looking on with fixed smiles. You torture yourself on whether to tip and the percentage thereof. Is there a service charge? "Oops! I left my glasses at home." There's your perfect excuse. Change collected, a trite thank you directed at mid-distance, and you push out of the pull door with a tight smile of agony. You were supposed to come out prettier!

22

The Holiday

Have you ever wondered at your mixed feelings over a family holiday? You are kind of excited. There is a hint of a misgiving though as to how the grand plan will pan out. The tone and tenor of a vacation changes with age. The driving seat begins to attract competition from your adult kids. What time should the day begin? Should you soak it all in or seek it all out? What exactly is worth what you invested into the break? Moods swing. Egos clash. You miss out on sights and sounds because of landslides, rain or poor teamwork. There are inconveniences, minor ones. The group begins to look and act like an amoeba: an uncertain move in one direction followed by a tentative roll in another. You begin to miss your washing machine and pan tea. Even your denture container calls out to you as does your express WiFi connection back home. The pet appears as an apparition. You paste a smile on the face, shake clear your head, and sit up straighter, telling yourself, *"Oh. come on! Fun takes work!"* The game just about picks up when someone comes down with stomach flu. The law of averages is kept up by a matching allergy make an appearance in another of the group. You lumber homewards in time, after a chain of hits and misses, lugging sacks of laundry and chronic photo poses in choking memory cards. Yay! You just lived up to the myth perpetuated by masses of humans hung up on picture perfect postcards. The morning after, you are finally alone. You log on to Facebook and begin uploading the deceptive frames. There you go, redrafting objective reality into memories that will narrate your kind of life story. Memory, after all, is elastic!

The Masculine

Have you ever felt uncomfortably masculine next to a properly feminine woman? A colleague, a friend, a neighbour perhaps. Smooth skin, floating limbs, and princess airs. She walks in, and you step back to offer her space. She enacts a lighter version of the spoilt child and you laughingly and gamely concede. She expresses her preferences under the garb of playful accusations, and you run to comply. Her butterfly presence is in a stark contrast to your no-nonsense, minimalistic, and grave substance. Your communication protocol with the world could not be more different. She pouts her way to the point; you cut to the chase. Values like punctuality, preparedness, penny watching place you both on either end of the spectrum. You blanch at any mention of being manipulative; she glories in the power of stealth seduction. She is always accompanied; you are frequently alone. She wilts and wanes; you are annoyingly weatherproof. She values the aesthetic deliverance she brings to humanity; you have a phobia of being mistaken for the Christmas tree. Gratitude is her banner; you are forever waving flags of independence and self-sufficiency. You privately think you are the more authentic, the smarter of the two. It makes you almost smug, therefore, when life presents her with a frog to kiss and you get the prince himself. Imagine your horror as you lower your lips for the affection you think you deserve…they nick on the spiny lycra of frog skin. Your eyes shoot open to stare after the feminal form, all languid and draped over the protective arm of what was, until now, a frog!

The Chastiser

Have you ever done something stupid, felt an idiot over it, then had the moronity rued and cautioned against by a near and dear one? They could have left you alone to stew for a while. But they have to be your Siamese twin, joined at the hips, responsible for your actions and words, your shareholder in the consequences. Why won't the world trust you to kick yourself adequately enough? After all, you do have your mummy voice sitting in the head, ever ready with its raised index finger and the tut-tut sound. You were born with a self-policing meter, keenly calibrated by schools, temples, and parents. In fact, you, in particular, just can't seem to stop being more human than the human! You go pulling the doors marked "push". In weak moments, you simply resort to your primitive self. There you go, stabbing both the up and down buttons on the lift. You regularly go on auto-pilot, mindfulness be damned! It takes just one driver to break the red light for you to follow suit. Your resolve to give away old clothes faces constant revision. A maniacal possessiveness overtakes you to gaze at your stock of dry fruits, homemade pickle, unused First Aid items, and rubber bands. You flip the lid with the maid, the Vodafone customer care guy, the parking attendant, the caddie even. Then you go hitting a wayward tee shot on the golf course. Furious and heartbroken at the duff, you swing your brand new driver on the fairway, taking a chunk out. The world promptly conspires to rub it in. A fellow golfer, friend, or even a life partner steps up to patronize and draw you away from the sin that is certain, apparently, to prompt the wrath of God.

25

The Privacy

Have you ever wondered at our very Indian clumsiness with privacy? While the cultivated world grows obsessive with absolute privacy as against merely fundamental, we happily trip along, trampling all over the very idea of confidentiality. "Have not seen Mrs. Bhambra in a while" is enough for a total lowdown on what exactly is keeping the lady away. "Poor thing, she is attending elderly neglect and abuse hearings in the court against her children. It is so sad!" Illnesses, business lows, affairs of the heart, travails of the children…all are grist to this delightfully secular, social mill. "What's the big deal?" is the general opinion. Life is a little bit messy for each and every one. Who does not go through ups and downs? Your binding duty is to share it all with the person you are currently in cosy conversation with, heads together and legs joined, knee touching knee. "This is just between you and me, but Tooky is in denial of his son's addiction, I think. Poor guy, it is such a nightmare. The family is going through a terribly harrowing time. Just keep it to yourself." And we do, to ourselves…well, self, add one more and the immediate family. There is not even a pretence around vital data such as age, weight, contact details, and cosmetic procedures in this country of tell-all. It is common for a consultant to loudly proclaim within hearing of his assistant and the waiting patients, "Make a note! Remind me to check up on Madam's tummy tuck next week!" And the gym trainer is not beyond discussing with you your broad female pelvis and those typical fat deposits, all under the poker gaze of the onlooking sweaty faces. We are disarming and charming at spilling to complete strangers…in the bus, on flights, at waiting rooms. While Europe chokes itself on an over-regulated privacy policy that threatens to cost the continent jobs, growth, and technological advancement, we are still struggling to tell privacy from piracy.

The Circuit

Have you ever had someone younger lunge at your knees? It can be destabilizing. On reflex mode, you stick your breech out and dip at the waist, getting the genuflecting frame on their shoulder blades with just the tips of your first three fingers. Garbled air exits the vocal cords. There is a self-conscious social flutter, and you both withdraw thankfully the very next moment. There! The deed is done. A time old tradition has been observed. There is community relief at this event establishing hierarchy. Also, core values of respecting elders, showering blessings, and committing to the tribe. All is in place, as it should be. Only the degree of stooping, the angle so to say, keeps rising, alarmingly so! Our rishis left clear instructions to stand facing our superior and then bend fully, crossing our hands to connect the left foot with our left hand and right with the right. Mirror image, remember! With the elder placing their right hand on our head, the circuit closed and the switch transferring his goodness to us, was essentially flipped on. Our spirit absorbed the elders' virtues and strength and wisdom and intellect. It was meant to be nurture at the soul level, transference of life experiences and good old energy. Hopefully, some concentrated lessons too. Now what good can we possibly be accruing from a guru's shin? A grandparent's calf? Or the thigh of an unsuspecting parent-in-law? Heaven help us the day we land on the groin. No wonder we are going cross-eyed with cultural confusion. The circuit has to close people!

27

The Decimal

Have you ever been struck by our spryness at rounding off decimals? Selectively. Exam aggregates, febrile readings, distances run or cycled are habitually rounded up. Electric meter readings, second-hand age of items being posted on OLX, weighing machine posts are routinely rounded down. And there is a qualifying word we use with these round declarations. The word is "about". It is also accompanied with a feigned amnesia. The act comes together in a predictable sequence. The brow furrows, and the eyes narrow while attempting an accurate recall. Your child's board-exam score will be about 93%. You would have cycled about 125 km. You are quite likely about 73 kg in weight. The house you bought five years ago would likely have cost you about 55 lakhs, all told. Little white lies, constitutionally covered under the freedom of speech. You are not, after all, gaining any unlawful benefit from these dressy admissions. You just want others to think better of you. We don't merely round off our numerals, we round off our deeds too. I have sat up studying all night, for instance, but I will whinge and whine my lack of preparation around friends so as to protect myself from their envious black eyes. I am sweating away in the kitchen but will smilingly refuse any offer of help from the guests in a magnanimous show of hospitality. I am tired and just not in the mood to attend an office function, but I round off the discomfort with a story of my alimentary canal tripping up. We cannot afford the decimals you see! Rounding off is statutory to social survival amongst us. Faces can't be lost. Backs must be covered!

<h1 style="text-align:center">28</h1>

<h1 style="text-align:center">The Mausoleum</h1>

Have you ever sat on a red sandstone bench under fluorescent foliage in a centuries-old mausoleum, overseen by an epileptic flyover? The marble cenotaphs smile knowingly at the madness outside the ruinous gates. Squirrels prance about. The birds go into paroxysms of hopping and chirping. The sonic trail of a plane lazes overhead, a train rumbles by, the lawn mower coughs up copious grass…this space awaits! Time seems to perch alongside. You slide off the seat and shift onto the shadowy grass. With a sigh, you lie back and gaze up at the blue. Birds glide over laden bushes, and the butterflies rise in spirals. Your skin hums to the cool ebb and flow of the breeze. If you sit still, you can hear the stoic ticking of time and the restful oasis bidding its while. It feels like home, a final touchdown. The flowers nod calculatedly, mocking at the honking hatred in traffic jams close by. Your rude phone planner spews an appointment with the dermatologist. The spell breaks. You make to leave, then fall back again. You are not done applying balm yet. The nose tickles; eyes sting; the heart brims over. You take a resolute step into the slapping sun only to retreat in haste. It makes sense to edge sideways around the edifice, looking for a way into its anchored womb. The iron grill is locked. You bang at it and rattle the metal. Oh no. It is not time yet!

The Wish

Have you ever felt a masked rage at having to hear as an aside, "I wish you had told me"? It is the smartest phrase in the lexicon of self-preservation. The speaker gets to kill four birds with a stone. He gets to digest his terror by blaming you and is able to add insult to injury while covering himself in glory! You have just woken up from deep sleep in the Second AC, for instance. Your muddled mind is struggling to accept that your handbag is missing. "I wish I had known you had kept it there, in plain sight," your sibling says helpfully. How many times have you been told this by a neighbour after a destructive thunderstorm: "I wish you had left the keys with me; I would have had the windows double-checked and latched." Another time, you decided not to take your parent's advice to store some water the night before an important interview. Now, having slept through the motor switch on time, beyond an hour, you are listening to your landlord pontificate, "I wish I had known you were to dress up formally today!" Is this not a very subtle form of victim blaming? The speaker clearly believes he could have helped matters by doing things differently. The world is not necessarily a fair place though. Bad things can and sometimes do happen to good people like you and me. Who are we helping by not commiserating? The thing to do when faced with someone already kicking themselves is to zip the lips. What we need to do thereafter is to set up schools of empathy and openness and then enrol in one! Have a heart now.

30

The Genes

Have you nursed a secret sense of genetic superiority over your spouse, laying claim thereby to the progeny's sharp intellect, great sense of humour, and dainty chins? Their wobbly teeth, over-pronated feet and nasal allergies you attribute to the other side of the family. Don't beat yourself up, though. It is not just your narrow, self-congratulatory, enmeshed self. This unshakeable belief in one's wholesome stock is nature's way of ensuring you stay affirmatively alive. It is quite the done thing, isn't it, to turn slowly but carefully to the spouse at the doctor's matter-of-fact query: "Anyone in the family with a history of diabetes?" This biologically zealous sentiment extends to aspects of life other than the mere physical. Let's say the kid goes missing a milestone or two in life and darn, it is that uncle of his with his bad influence. Sporting glory, sharp features, broad foreheads, clear skin are all keenly contested and claimed by both the paternal and maternal clans. Prematurely grey hair, thunder thighs, bunions …no thank you! And how come every dinner table in every human home resounds with sagas of beautiful great grandmothers, self-made grandfathers, gritty family survival, tenacious times, lost treasures, and slightly distant but generic invincibility. There is no knowing what creative liberties have been taken in these inter-generational Chinese whispers, but the stories are crucial since they celebrate qualities important to the identity of the kinsmen and the culture. What, therefore, is more important of the two? Veracity of family lore or its inspirational kick? Would you believe the genealogical data unearthed by @Ancestry or continue to draw strength from your great grandmother's fabled revolt against female feticide?

II

SILENT SCREAM

The Cosmetics

Have you ever wondered at the long-suffering lipsticks and nail enamels awaiting conclusive disposal on your dressing table? They have turned fickle with time, flaky and functional by turns, but you cannot bring yourself to release them. We are brought up to maintain a vice-like grip on our possessions. Many an Indian heart has wept at having to throw away expired medicines. "Are you sure your knee is no longer hurting? Here, pop this paracetamol; it is about to expire. Why waste it?!" Our cabinets, drawers, shelves sag under the weight of drying, congealing, caking material that we fear might come in handy one day. That body lotion bottle you have tapped, rinsed out, squeezed to death still sits for the final scooping out of the inaccessible lid. No one knows what to do with that aged organic toner, but it awaits pick up; the bottle is full to the brim, making it utterly ineligible for throwing. Some nail paints have split into solvent and sediment; there are lipsticks that scrape the mouth, but maybe they can someday be mixed with other shades and put to use. What if the children needed face paint for school shows sometimes? They could then prove useful as markers and binders…let them stay. Eye shadows, blush ons, mascaras are the cosmetic equivalent of dinosaurs. No one knows their life expectancy. They just live on, degrading and oxidizing with time. There are also our array of applicators and nail care arsenal, lying tidy in smart but yellowing packaging. The covers may crack but our resolve won't let them be opened until absolutely needed. While the First and Second Worlds debate ethical disposal of chemical products complete with planetary respect, what are we doing with those pale stick on bindis that disappear on our sepia skins?!

32

The Donkey

Have you niggled yourself occasionally that you failed in life on the projection front? That you remained a donkey at work rather than a preening peacock. All plodding, no shoo-shaaa-show. You were not street-smart enough to give your boss a peek into your late-night homework and notes that you scribbled frantically in the care before the traffic lights turned green. You were raised to believe that hard work paid. No one said anything about its qualifying visibility, though! You laboured three days over a near flawless report, for instance, but there it was, your plain plastic cover tucked out of sight under your rival's ethnic themed folder on the Vice President's table. While you were racing back from a last-minute administrative tie up, he was rounding off the "With your blessings" routine. Your sincere interactive sessions with your juniors paled in comparison with his resourceful hobnobbing at the executive table. While you flailed to keep up a sputtering stream of organizational loyalty, he flew on the Asics of unadulterated self-interest. You kicked yourself every September when report cards were being rolled out. Why didn't you update your boss more regularly? Why did you get boxed into a hole? Why did you get defensive when being criticized? Why didn't you raise your nose from the grindstone once in a while? Then along came the man himself one day, asking you to stand in for him at a graduation speech while he went globetrotting to pitch business proposals to singular multinationals. He tossed you his prepared text, "Here, should you want to use it. The topic is: Hard work does not speak for itself. You do!"

33

The Remedy

Have you ever blamed a compliment on your saree for the blob of *malai kofta* curry you dropped on the pallu? The evil eye! While you stare aghast at the greasy spot, your admirer's expansiveness transforms into guilty dismay. "I should have gushed less!" You recover shakily to assure "It is alright. I will have it dry-cleaned," but the damage is done. There you sat another time at your aunt's breakfast table. While she oohed and aahed at your trendy new outfit, her wretched beagle sat chomping the beaded tassel trailing the floor under the dining table! As a rule, Indians have an uneasy equation with admiration. We are spasmodic both at giving and receiving it. How often have you drooled over a friend's silver bracelet only to be hastily assured it is a cheap imitation? She fears your envy! Or doesn't want you to feel any lesser. "What a gorgeous bag!" you exclaim. The wearer splutters, "Oh, it is very old; a hand me down from an aunt." If sounding ungracious helps save mishaps, so be it. We must be the world's most co-morbid race. We acknowledge envy exists and guard ourselves with mantras, chillies, limes, prayers, and charms. We spit, make frantic signs, rip white rags into seven strips, swirl camphor smoke, and emanate a range of audio effects to banish ill will. Families store and apply these formulas as traditional, customized arsenal. A runny tummy? Out springs a fistful of rock salt. Falling grades? Water and kumkum. Emotional rejection? Wait, we have the perfect poultice of mustard seeds. And the all-time favourite Indian domestic deterrent to rival the Tsar Bomba? A black dab from the adoring eye.

The Seat

Have you heard of any other nationality that "keeps" place for a friend with a handkerchief, a card, a handbag, a water bottle, a brochure, a key ring, and sometimes merely a protective hand? "Save a place for me, alright. I am nearly there!" The friend is in fact just starting out from home. You sit there in the meanwhile, the skin growing steadily thicker. It begins with a confident dumping of the handbag on the chair next to yours. As the hall begins to fill up, your crafty talents come to the fore. You avoid meeting accusatory eyes, several spots in the mid space seemingly holding you spellbound. You disown the bag initially, even giving it annoyed looks! As the audience begin squeezing into the fast-filling seats around you, you pile your sunglasses and some gum on to the bag to add to its proprietorial appearance. An assertive voice insists on your attention from the shadowy interiors of the theatre, "Excuse me, is someone sitting here?" Your throat directs a garbled response at the sound, "Washroom! Restroom! Just. Yes. Someone." A trickle of sweat slowly begins to meander down your temple as you crane your neck towards the closest door, pretending an indulgent impatience. Even a Delhiite can't stretch an ingenious game of entitlement beyond a point. From the corner of your eye, you catch sight of the organizer, approaching at a clip. Stumped and stuck, you try cracking the whip on your mulish mind when a heavy human mass tramples on your toes, half falling across your rigid body onto your Burberry glasses. The soft crack of the expensive buy drowns in your pal's loud laugh. "Sorry, man, killer diversion! These VIPs and their 'lal batti' really need to go."

35

The Godrej

Have you as a child had an exciting fascination with the Godrej almirah back home? The keys to it would be in burglar-proof places such as under the grand maternal pillow! There would be an almost ceremonial air to picking the right one from the bunch and placing it in the hole. The pregnant pause after the click would rival the anticipation of Alibaba and his forty thieves. A smart dip of the handle and the doors would clang open with a resounding wrench. You would survey the fragrant interiors over the adult owner's shoulder. A three-decade-old stock of the 'Moti' and 'Mysore Sandal' soaps. The pink, satin, cushioned tea cosy with its English doll. There would be beautiful bits of treasures placed there for security and longevity. Grandfather's fountain pen. A carved walking stick. Several bunches of old letters held together with fading strings. A Japanese fan, a bolt of Malaya fabric, a pair of cabin slippers gifted by a Canadian relative. And then there would be another key. To the locker! With its treasure of your silver baby jewellery…the rattle, the anklets, the bowl and spoon and glass, and the silver urn in which would be placed crisp paper money on your special days. It gave you a piquant sense of security, the cupboard with its vault-like presence in your little world. *We are rich; we have nice things*, you hugged the thought to yourself. Now several years later, you stare searchingly at the piece of furniture, frowning and sad at the used-up space, wondering where its deluxe hauteur has gone. *What was the big deal exactly?!*

36

The Osmosis

Have you marvelled at our osmotic ability to flow in and out of each other's spaces and faces? We appropriate each other in shared confines as a matter of course. Achhhoo! Heaven help you if home remedies for cold do not come crashing at your aching head from all directions! You demonstrated a lack of foresight on your foreign trip by not purchasing golf shoes? More than one compatriot will want to know the reason why. "You should have tried them on there. Here you are combing Sports 365 now. Why didn't you?" And please don't go losing your cool with anyone. You will be patronized by the object of your ire from a moral high ground. "Hey, come on, don't get upset over such a small thing! I am sorry, ok? It was not my intention to hurt you." The world indeed is our family! And we hate letting anyone try coping by themselves. Say you messed up a golf shot one day? Assurance will march up in abundance. "Don't worry! The ball has gone a bit left but the distance is quite good!" You are stewing over a personal loss? "Cheer up! It could have been far worse." You just sat through a life-threatening diagnosis? "So sad, but it is all karma," someone is sure to point out. Judgments, assurances, advice, words of caution… they all flow like air and water and fake news. You admired something on a person? "Here, I will tell you where to get it. In fact, why don't you take this?" The world wonders why India does not invent or create or discover in proportion to its population. When would we? We don't leave each other alone long enough!

The Napkin

Have you struggled with the pretentious existence of napkins in your life? A truly satisfying, thorough, squeaky scrub. Have you experienced one ever? The squares instead leave you high and dry, the extremities hollering silently for good old water. Take the tea napkin. One fourth is adorned with a dainty flower, another chunk is lost to the lace, and you have a fig leaf sized surface to brandish over your soiled bits. And oh, those vain rolls of spotless fabric, delicately tucked into bejewelled holders; they are the dining table's ivory tusks, purely nominal and wholly non-functional. A few diners are lion-hearted enough to smudge the chaste beauties with yellow and green food stains. The paper napkins that materialize on subdued summons barely console, what with their overly-glazed surfaces skimming your spots uselessly. But of course, there is the thicker variety, roomier and patterned. Their expertise, unfortunately, is in spreading the splatter evenly so it is less visible. The trendy but coarse paper probably scoops it all into the pores, who is to say! And better have a lint picker standing by should you be desperate enough to swipe your face with one of those tissues one balmy day. Humanity also awaits the perfect napkin holder. One that does not strike dread in the guest's heart as it approaches ceremoniously besides a paneer tikka platter. People hold their breath as two fingers stretch out tentatively; there is a tug, the tray bobs dangerously, and, like a pack of cards, the napkins fan out to land with a hush on the floor. Water rinse or lick clean! Wash cloths or paper towels! We haven't begun with the orifices yet.

38

The Drive

Have you ever sat turning a nervous wreck besides a self-confident driver? He treats the road as his private estate, hurtling down flyovers and blaring through congestions. You inhale and exhale, alternating between a trance and a prayer. There is an ego at stake! Like everyone who takes to the wheels, he considers himself an above average driver! Your rear-view mirror just nicked a glistening grey Ciaz. A hiss escapes your lips; you stuff it back into your drying mouth. You bite back a gasp of terror at the approaching roundel. There is a bedlam of impatience there. Horns honk, tyres screech, brakes protest. A Delhi Police crane cuts in authoritatively, and this time you mewl in anticipation, drawing an injured look from the driving seat. The toes ache with their flex and dip on imaginary controls down there. You stare out of the window, rigid with suspense and wanting desperately to take over the wheel; you are carrying your driving licence as a standby, just in case the gentleman finds an occasion to indulge in a drink. The vehicles are converging at the red light, jostling to get ahead. You squeeze your eyes and clench the jaw, dreading the sound of scraping metal as the cars inch forward cheek by jowl, no one willing to give up an inch of space. The departure from home was based on an optimistic estimate of travel time. Quite abruptly, the Grand Prix ends and out jumps the man, all triumphant and validated. This was not just about getting from one place to another. It was a race, a chase, a dramatic combat...a display of masculinity learnt over thousands and thousands of years!

39

The Gift

Have you ever, in a fit of exuberance, given away a nice gift only to regret it later? Now it comes back in insistent flashes. Oh my God, that was such an elegant stole; I could have used it myself or given it to family. The business of gifting is such a marshland, you rethink every step. Two boxes of savouries come from somewhere. On a particularly rushed day, you pick up one on your way to a gathering. Imagine your horror when you open the remaining tin later to find the richest, dry fruits-filled creations inside. You are shattered at the loss! It is not just in giving, it is in receiving too that we get taken in at times. An acquaintance leaves behind a bag that you give only a cursory look. You don't know them well enough after all, so you acknowledge their gesture and bundle the fabric back hastily. Some days later, lightning strikes at a high-end outlet where something similar is quoted for way beyond anything you would have imagined the lady spending. You rush home to confirm! While one half of you feels toasty, the other half is chilled to the bones at the thought of an equivalent return. Matching a gift with the potential receiver's status, taste, and history with you and the occasion…this art is learnt gradually. The resourceful keep a look out for bargains on items purely meant for passing around. Shopkeepers will sometimes ask outright, "You want this for yourself or to give away?" The jury is out there on whether anyone any longer gets a particularly big kick out of what they give or receive. Or is it that proverbial habit that on not being challenged becomes a necessary chore, the recipient being as blasé as the gift giver.

40

The Auntyji

Have you wondered at the dubious connotation to this word: auntyji?! Does it convey respect, really? Or is it received as a put down, well, almost? Auntyji! A dowdy creature of the female species with a tired and balloon-like uterus, she depends on her husband for two square meals a day and upon her kids to give meaning to her life. Her appalling lack of style is matched by her annoyingly middle-class aspirations for her family. Husband should live long, and kids should get into good jobs and then find suitable partners and soon give her grandchildren. Auntyji is boring, thrifty, and paranoid. She is also interfering and nosy, suggesting things to eat and forever on the prowl mode, stalking her child's friends, searching and destroying any evil eye threatening to befall the apples of her eyes. What gives her a high are pickle recipes and stain removers! Having spent her prime years putting her own health, comfort, and growth last, she now faces irrelevance and contempt. "Get yourself a life, auntyji!" While the potent young and the productive adults ride the rollercoaster of life on their way to fame and fortune and fulfilment, auntyji gathers moss, consistently predictable and living by proxy. If anything, there is a half-ashamed annoyance at her taking up space and consuming resources. "You want to learn to dance? At your age? Auntyji!" Or "Now that your children are grown and gone, how about you start visiting the temple more often?" And "Your wifely and motherly roles are done; please contribute to the community now." Not much is spoken or recorded of her immense contribution to keeping alive a tightly held, secure, culturally rich social fabric. If anything, she has a new and uber-powerful enemy: Modern Psychology's "Science of Blaming Mom for All Evil."

41

The Judgment

Have you frequently had to play the lawyer for yourself? You chart life's course defending and justifying and explaining yourself. People around you refuse to grant you the fundamental right to be imperfect. Your heart is crying out for approval and affirmation from your ecosystem 24x7, but what echoes back are judgments. Everybody says, "Nobody is perfect," but in their hearts, they think they darn nearly are, and they most certainly expect perfection from you. The fall out is a constant fear of being thought less of. In anticipation of disapproval, you make statements like, "Yes, my daughter is a dancer *but* she majored in Maths!" Or, "We don't live with my parents-in-law, *but* no, there is no fight or anything." And, "My son is thirty and says he is not ready for marriage, *but* I have done my duty by facilitating suitable matches for him." The disclaimer keeps growing longer in the hope that it keeps us above blame in our own heads and in the minds of others. The fun begins when the formula is applied to others. It suddenly sounds different. "She keeps a lovely house, *but* is bipolar, I believe!" Or worse still, "She is very smart, *but* she overshadows her husband completely." Sometimes, "He is professionally sound *but* suffers from a glad eye." Could it be that our ancient wise taught us this trick of imperfect perfection so as to deflect the world's envy? There is international heartburn as it is over our *Anarkali Disco Chali* song, our *Palak Patta Chat* recipe, and our *Juhi ka Attar* perfume. We'd do better to continue to pass judgments on each other lest the world find out how awesome we really are!

42

The Nickname

Have you sheepishly risen from your CEO's chair to grin at the sound of your childhood name? "Bitti!" the voice envelopes you excitedly. It is your neighbour of thirty-five years. "Poontie!" You grin back broadly, scanning your work space slyly through the closing door, just to know how far the sound carried. Phew! The ambivalent power of nicknames. At the school reunion of twenty years, they are all there in their trappings of success. "Where the hell is Patto? Hey, Diggo! Teetoo! Any idea guys?" The heads that shake in the negative are many. There is Goonn, Tillu, Chiki and Meeku, not to mention Rippu, Gullu, and Tota. The names reach out from the past to haunt. A highly formal and uniformed event comes to mind, at which two Generals face each other, their smiles shinier than their brass. "Chottu!" And booms the other "Jazz!" Nicknames cut through our social armour to scoop out the child within us. They are reminders of a time when we were vulnerable and dependent and cherished. For an immediate sense of familiarity and connection, there is nothing like a "Kooky" or a "Binny" or a "Jeeta". Words carry tons and tons of invisible baggage that shape not just our thoughts but material outcomes. *Pinni, Sukku,* and *Gogu* are about accessibility and that all important human connection. Let's reclaim our nicknames today and break down the walls and barriers keeping us from each other! Amplify camaraderie, shall we, and take our association to a grand new digital scale with names like *Bebo, Lolo, Aalu, Chirkoot, Faffy,* and *Mimi*!

The Tea

Have you wondered at all the fuss around brewing of the tea? You are in awe of the talk over flavours and timbre and body and aroma. The fancy tea packages, those silk tassels, dainty sachets, neat infusers and elegant teaware…you would like to participate wholeheartedly in the classy tea club. There is something to that deeply ingrained image in our heads, of paisley furnishings in a living room with a robust fireplace, a greyhound flopped alongside a well-worn rocking chair, a horse or two neighing outside on the misty moor, and you pouring gently brewed tea into an English porcelain cup. There is a plate of scones with jam and clotted cream waiting. You are Catherine Earnshaw, and Heathcliff is on his way, having made his fortune, riding hard to make it before the tea turns cold! There is Oolong, Green, White, Assam, Sri Lankan, Earl Grey, Sencha, and Gyokuro teas. There are brands to choose from such as Tetley, Yorkshire, Bigelow, Lipton, Dilmah, Twinings, Tata, Taj, Red Label. There are custom methods to brewing tea. You steep, you do not over-boil, you get the water and milk proportion just right, and you portion the proper amount of tea leaves. Most of the enlightened, world-weary folks are very particular about their tea. They like to give precise instructions or will hover over the process to get their cup just so. Then one day, you enter an Armed Forces Mess as a guest. A waiter arrives bearing tea on a velvet covered tray. The beverage is out of this world. You have never tasted anything like it. You call for the cook. "Madam, I took water, milk, tea bag, and fresh ginger altogether, boiled it hard and good, and simply strained. Sugar to taste! Oh yes, the tea bag was standard purchase from the Army Canteen."

44

The Funsultant

Have you sat alone in a darkened room, a tight chest keeping you company? The feeling is odd because you count yourself lucky. Life has been good to you, yet there are unplanned, involuntary stabs of a profoundly sad stillness that you slip into at odd times during the day: outside in a party lawn, twinkling with fairy lights, surrounded by soft chatter and the clink and cascade of social bonhomie; in a hospital waiting room, the digital monitor pinging turns; right in the middle of a friend's animated chatter; strapped up in the beautician's chair waiting for her to select an instrument of choice. The sudden suspension comes, hanging over you, tentative and watchful, then you whisk yourself out to get on with things on hand, all waiting to be done. A wellness epidemic, after all, has taken over the world! There is tremendous pressure to constantly stay upbeat. But you glimpse them in other eyes too, hiding behind the selfie smiles, those normal emotions of anger, sadness, anxiety, and uncertainty. While you shiver with the consequent aloneness to the depths of your selfhood, the world goes about talking of Chief Happiness Officers. Funsultants do brisk business, enforcing compulsory fun. You better be seen to be happy! There is no let-up in this conspiracy of clowning. Where does a person stomp with rage, howl his agony, express his misgivings, lament their losses, grieve over the normal wear and tear of human life? That space for authenticity has all but shrunk. You better not be moody when you can shake your booty!

45

The Ball

Have you any idea the power of a dimpled ball less than two inches in diameter and not even fifty grams in weight? This spherical mass brings men to their knees. It is shocking, the level of their intimacy! A golfer will plead with, curse at, swear eternal gratitude to that ball he just whacked. Watch him follow the flight, frozen in suspense, a stream of syllables tumbling out of a petrified mouth. "Go, go, go, go. Oh, no… you went left yesterday too. This is not done!" And, "Is she back? Is she back? No, no, no…she can't have gone out of bounds. What is wrong with you?" Some go up in unison, the caddie joining the chant, "She will go, she will go… past the metal frame, skim through the water, bounce off the hard sand…there she goes, climb, climb, climb, you witch…aah…on the green!" The ball is an equivalent of Farrah Fawcett's iconic red swimsuit poster; it reduces them to chumps. It is Buffy, the vampire slayer. Grown, accomplished, perfectly sane men pluck and plod and pick through trees and bushes, slicing, stabbing, and punching in vain. The ball goads them on, dancing in defiance, leaving slumped shoulders, despairing spirits, and shaking heads in her wake. Of course! The women play too. Between fighting their Johnny-come-lately self-consciousness and the occasional patronising from their born-to-golf partners, they watch and marvel at how little it takes to undo a mother's work!

46

The Tip

Have you ever invested more in a tip than strictly necessary? You could have just left that change and walked out, basking in fullness and goodness. But no. That would be against your grain. It is customary to have the upper hand, be smarter than the other, get a good deal, outwit those fellows. Letting anyone get the better of us constitutes harakiri. So, there you go, the shrewd, seasoned, streetwise local, fretting over tips. And you never seem to get it right! You come away feeling either foolishly generous or a downright penny-pincher. You try hard! You research tipping practices around the world. Hell, how do they calculate it in the USA? No, 20% is too much. What does the fine print on the bill say? Did they include service charges? Why is the waiter cracking up, smiling? Is he bending backwards towards a fat tip? Why is my family glaring at me across the restaurant table? Are they annoyed I left too much, or are they feeling ashamed of my cheese-paring? Where is my calculator? This foxy footwork of yours finds more forums to flit on. You just loaded up a grocery bag at the INA market. The shop owner nudges a coolie along. "*Twenty or thirty,*" you ask yourself. *No, no, it is their job! I bought stuff worth thousands. Thank you, bhaiya ji!*" thinking thus, you flash your saccharine smile instead. At the red light, you are asking yourself, "*When did service become a luxury? It is my entitlement,*" when a beggar woman taps on your car window. "Rot in hell, you miser! Remember, what goes around, comes around!" she hoots after your dodging tail lights.

47

The Blessing

Have you ever been told by a toothy mouth in a wobbly voice, "Son! I have nothing to give you but my blessings!" You bite your lips, frown delicately, then stretch the lips to reveal the pearlies with a thin indulgence. *"The 50,000/- EMI is killing me. How many blessings would it take!"* you feel ashamed at the thought. Blessings, tradition says, are all we should need. Blessings, after all, are what we are most lavish with. Watch us give and receive them…with more aplomb than the French roll their wine. Whoever calls us a nation of the closefisted has not seen us lay it on thick. "Go, give up your youthful life for the country, child; our blessings are with you!" And, "You are struggling to set up home in a strange, racist nation; take our blessings." And, "Has there been a life-threatening diagnosis? Worry not! We will bless you." Also, "Can't pitch in with that loan, but here, keep our blessings." The most common, "No, we have no package for delivery, but do convey our blessings!" We use every medium available to propagate our benedictions. The social networks, ethereal airwaves, snail mail are all clogged with invocations. The mindless frequency of their perfunctory discharge does raise a question, though. Who takes charge of the blessings after their grand pronouncements? Someone has to own them, right? Ah, those precious blessings! No one tells us that their manifestation is directly proportional to our participation. Mere counting them is not enough!

48

The Doomsayer

Have you, our national and typical intolerance for mistakes and failures? Akin to lactose intolerance of the west? All events, major and minor must go smoothly. You get panic attacks if someone you are invested in messes up. You resent friends and family for not anticipating, for not putting enough thought into your combined projects, for costing you grief you had not slotted in. "How could they be so careless? They should have known the road is terrible!" Or, "I warned them about the holiday rush!" And, "You should have organized your papers better!" There is an absolute inability to accept human weaknesses or allow others a compassionate space to lick their wounds in peace. Blame has to be apportioned, guilt established, and judgement passed. We have nil stomach or stamina or strength for things going wrong. It helps that while we forget our own flubs, our memory remains razor sharp about other peoples' glitches. Why does our system hum with so much disapproval and criticism by the smug doomsayers? There are reasons. One, we grow up with sharp notions of right and wrong, done and not done, acceptable and unacceptable. Second, given our flaky civic structure and rickety infrastructure, the cost of blotches feels terrifyingly unaffordable. What do we do? We become control freaks. No risks. No trying any off beaten roads. No loss of face in particular. No wastage of resources, heaven forbid. We avoid mistakes like the plague, and in the bargain, learn nothing new.

49

The Retirement

Have you drawn up a bucket list ever? Perhaps you live with a sense of invincibility and immortality. Others die, not you, not yet at any rate. Of course, in your heart of hearts, you know there is that moment and the destined day, inching closer. You may even have idly flirted with the thought of how it will all end, but one doesn't dwell, it might bring bad luck. So here you are, living with an underlying belief in a grander tomorrow. If and when it comes! The brighter, better tomorrow. We all suffer from the disease of 'someday'. One day, you are going to shed those kilos. Someday, you will play your heart out on the saxophone. Not too far in the future, there will be a tryst with the reindeer on a glacial river in Iceland. You will write that book. The golfing hole-in-one is just waiting to happen. You will not go without giving back to society. You have to make up to your parents yet. Spiritual evolution beckons. Your children still need you. And there is just this little, niggling matter of retirement. "Once we retire and settle down, I am going to do it all!" Meanwhile, the free radicals are taking over your cells, your organs are preparing to overdraw on their functional reserve, and you see the crepe-like skin on other necks, but your own face still gives a plump and smooth illusion in the indoor lighting over your mirror. You really should make that list before the jowls begin to sag. Soon, there won't be enough time! So why on earth would you put off being alive and young until you retire?!

50

The Spam

Have you realized how redundant Google has made you in your human interactions? Keep your life transforming *gyan* to yourself, for one. Everybody has it on their fingertips. Your niece seems to struggle in a relationship, and you decide to offer your expertise! She half listens to your anxious recipe with her off-centre smile telling you to shut up. She has read it all on Google already. As the family senior, you delicately launch the birds and the bees talk, pompous at your progressive move, but hear, "Look, patriarch, we know the theory. Nobody is getting pregnant, and there is no STD happening. Ya, ya, ya, it is under control, emotional scarring and all. This is a private domain. Hands off. End of discussion." A marriage proposal is afoot with a family young. The beau and the beauty have put technology to good use; they have checked each other out and virtually made up their minds. Now your much-awaited cue comes. "Please step into your uncle slot of the picture frame and smile into the camera. Thank you! Get off the dais please." The professional relationships rate even higher on redundancy. Patients may come primed to distrust their doctor, having Googled their medical condition in advance. Students may expect just the context from their teachers rather than academic content; they know it all from Google. The problem is of filters. Of cultural reference points. And a personal, emotional investment. Google gives you what you want. It is a view delivered without the responsibility or accountability of real, flesh and blood people who are, for now, just spam. Celebrate your spam-hood while it lasts, folks. Spam too is set to be a thing of the past!

51

The Family

Have you had trouble reconciling disagreement and family love? People who love you have to listen to you. You have to be together in tandem, at all times, about everything. There is presumed to be a fundamental fault line in families that allow dissenting voices and tangential views! A good family moves through life, all sticky and sugary a la Karan Johar's "family above all else" template. "Ma, I want to be known only by my first name!" would technically qualify as rejection of the family. "I can't believe you are using a word like 'habshi'; it is so racist" is clearly at odds with the family's legacy of superior genes. "Listen Pa, I can't do family, six days in a row" has to be high on the clannish scale of blasphemy. "How could you enrol in the scuba diving course without consulting us?" is disbelief at the implied disloyalty. Healthy families do everything together: movies, trips, events, and coffee. They are like garam masala, a single aroma crush of spectacular, stand-alone spices…highly functional and rich at the cost of their distinctive uniqueness. Imagine a family that looked like a masala container with space for cardamom, clove, cinnamon and black pepper. A circle of safe space that permitted thrashing around, identity exploration, risk-taking. Who is to say what outcomes would sally forth were we to define protocols for such supportive circles!

52

The Enamel

Have you ever put off painting your nails too long? The paint dullens, the cuticles begin to peep, and the chips propagate. The energy of those apologetic fingertips is not too removed from that of a sink full of dirty dishes. Unseemly, energy sucking, and malaise causing. You could be wearing your fanciest of outfits, but the patchy nails dim your dazzle. They nag, and you try to curl and shrink them out of sight. It begins to feel like a drag; painting nails becomes the dithering equivalent of a dental visit, to be put off until absolutely necessary. Pushed, you might hastily paint a camouflage coat on top of the mottled mess, but the result is hardly airy. You let another week or so go by, lugging the layered claws. "My nails are looking so terrible; there was no time to do them," you might voice a sheepish defence to a friend. "Let's get a manicure and a pedicure and be done with it," you eventually come to the conclusion. At the parlour, you take eighteen minutes to select a shade, and the spirit begins to lift with the first swipe. Who would have known the insidious role enamel plays in our lives! The pretty toffee pearl colour brightens you up. You stretch your toes and fingers, admiring the neat glow from different angles. Several compliments come your way over the following days. You find solace from raging gloom and bleak thoughts. Voila! You shine. Every now and then. And there are the bare nailed, wonder what they do!

53

The Pitstop

Have you been in the pit stop ever? It is the most interesting space to be in. It has neither the ceremony of the starter hut nor the excitement of the finish line. But there is drama, a palpable air of part relief at the distance covered and part anxiety at the ground to come. There is a muted celebration, a tentative relief. Water bottles are topped up, and bananas do the rounds. Energy bars and hard candies are exchanged. A packet or so of ORS might be ripped. That stop is also a photo op! And yet, when successful summit climbs and channel lengths and Formula 1 records are celebrated, there is barely a mention of the men and material that sustained the heroes at the halfway point. No talk of that poignant moment when a flagging human spirit was resuscitated with a Glucovita Bolt or a quick realignment of the gears or a change of the worn wheels or a *josh* talk. But for the pit stop crew, many a dream would have sunk with the night. It takes a special kind of sympathetic adrenaline to be ready in the wings. It takes stress by association and an acute participation by proxy. It takes heart and patience and respect for the performer. We all have our Lollypop man to guide us in and out of our recharge stops. A friend, a parent, a significant other, a teacher, a mentor. In life, as in a race, half is done at any given time and the remaining half, yet to come!

54

The Parrot

Have you ever thrown water at someone's pet parrot because he ignored you? You just fed him soaked almonds that he picked clean with his beak, the tiny red tongue bobbing behind the nut. You watched the speed demolition, expecting to be rewarded by a whistle of gratitude! But the bird gives you a dismissive squawk after confirming there are no more nuts coming. Miffed, you empty out your arsenal of sounds and funny faces, "Mithu! Poppat! Oye! Here! Listen!" You want the bird to cackle and cluck talk with you, but he turns away to dip his feathers in the bowl of water kept inside the cage. The green feathers shiver and shake off the drops, and the bird sinks his beak under the fanned span. Your voice begins to peter out at his indifference, and you are about to give up. "Madam, try Marathi! His owner speaks to him in Marathi," the caretaker suggests helpfully. "Aaple naav kahe?" you make a feeble attempt. "Mi Poppat, mi Poppat," the parrot screeches in excitement. You cast about for some long-forgotten Marathi phrases. "Tu kassa aahes?" Pat comes the rejoinder, "Mi theek aahe!" You are over the moon. You have always known you had this natural, God-given ability to connect with the animals. Satisfied to the core, you can't wait to see the bird again the next morning. You approach the cage, an ear-splitting grin in place, wondering why the caretaker will not look you in the eye. "Sahib murakh aahe!" shrieks Poppat.

55

The Bad

Have you wondered at how small your fan club is? You think of yourself as an OK person. You are quite self-sufficient, you don't complain, and you are fairly together, yet there is a pervasive suspicion that, well, you may not be guilty of popularity. "Laugh and the world laughs with you; cry and you cry alone," you were taught. "The world belongs to those who study," they told you. "Work is the remedy to all ills," you remember reading somewhere. "Time is money. Be your own person and live by your convictions. Only small minds discuss people. You owe it to yourself to realize your highest potential. Honour the memories of your ancestors and gurus. Be exemplary in all you do." In addition to milk and a high protein food, this was the essential diet you were raised on. You did it all. You toed the line. You kept your word. You were on time everywhere. You took initiative. You burnt the midnight oil. Hell, where are the cheering crowds now? Who is looking out for you? Perhaps they didn't want to give you a big head with direct praise and adulation! Something is off, but you are not quite sure what. At the university reunion some months later, you get into a debate with your mentor and professor of Philosophy on human interactions. "You idiot, don't you know imperfect is the new perfect. You don't have friends because you are too good to be true. Badass is the new sexy, didn't you know?!"

The Line

Have you ever switched rows only to regret it a moment later? You are at the railway station, in queue to buy a ticket. Two lines of impatient, hot, and humid folks are snaking along. You feel your particular column is dragging. Having made a quick calculation, you deftly shuffle to the faster one. But what's this, the file you left behind suddenly starts cruising. Another time, you do this to yourself at the toll booth. You scan the traffic at all the kiosks, taking care to pick the lightest. But just as you are pulling up, pleased as punch, all the longer series start clocking fast and furious while you remain stuck behind a tedious truck. Sick at heart with all the misfortune life seems to put on you, you snarl silently as the customer ahead counts the change in slow motion at the mall checkout. Be it the movies, the food court, the petrol pump, the bank…it happens over and over. You begin to think of yourself as the victim. How do you end up in the slowest moving line of them all? The boredom, the stress of keeping the smart alecks from cutting in, the sheer fatigue of shifting from one foot to the other…has anyone worked out the magic formula? How does one beat the queueing system? Anyone study the queueing theory? Help! If there is anything worse than waiting in a line, it is waiting in the wrong line!

57

The Book

Have you carted the book "I'm OK, You're OK" for years without having gone beyond page 29? You lug it around on long trips, telling yourself you will read it on the flights and the drives. The intention is present and given: the book is a must read. It was on New York Time's bestseller list, people talk about it, and the book cover does invite you in. But all the song and dance around it also leaves you with the feeling that you have almost, nearly, quite fully absorbed the essence of the tome. You are going to read it first-hand one day, that does not change! The entire dose, you tell yourself, chapter by chapter, page by page. As a matter of fact, you pull it out every now and then, stare at it, and save it back with care. Ditto for "The 7 Habits of Highly Effective People" and "Born to Win" and "Zen and the Art of Motorcycle Maintenance" and "Think and Grow Rich" and "The Power of Positive Thinking". Everybody owns these books and keeps them within reach, but nobody has read them entirely! They do, however, nod vigorously with that knowing smile when the titles come up in conversations. In time, the bestsellers start yellowing and disappear inside deep boxes. They resurface during home moves and spring cleanings, but you cannot bring yourself to give them away. So, they lie there, gathering dust and turning brittle while you get busy buying new, unread bestsellers to add to this pile. Maybe they should change the worthiness index of a book from "bestselling" to the "most finished"!

58

The Leverage

Have you ever run sticky fingers up a dewy and chilled bottle of water just so you could get some of the gooey-ness off? You put the drops that would have gone waste to good use! You were brought up to value resources. You make the most of what is available, the free fringe benefits in particular. Who is going to pay a tourist guide his exorbitant fees, for instance? Let's tag along with the foolishly extravagant group that has and eavesdrop. Save money and pinch some *gyan* that way! At the Taj Mahal another time, they are selling bright red shoe covers for INR 20, but they are good as new after one revolution around the monument. *Let's use a second-hand pair*, you tell yourself, *why waste?* You walk past the sales table right up to the dustbin and fish out the best covers from the discarded lot. At a foreign town once, it is a while before lunch time, and you could use a snack. You catch sight of a food store offering sample bites for free! The next fifteen minutes, you chomp with a taster's analytical expression, and after some deep thought and several calories downed, you walk out, shaking your head in gentle regret. Others should try matching us on returns on investment (ROI)! As a rule for instance, we don't use the touristy photographer. We watch from the corner of our eye and rapidly move into the spots he uses for our smart camera works of art. And hey, have you ever been adventurous enough to ride a freezing cold, mountain road? Get behind a public truck carrier, the warm exhaust will keep you cosy! Leverage! See an entrance? Enter.

59

The Fatigue

Have you ever been paid the ultimate Indian compliment: "You are just like family!" It doesn't get any more special than this. Family is the touchstone. "Just like family" is a euphemism for a "no matter what" commitment. You arrive on time for family. You book tickets for them. You are bound to fetch and carry for them. You arrange for their meals. You juggle your schedule to fit them in. You join them in group activities even if they don't excite you personally. You are accountable for their health. You take them shopping and sightseeing. You get them gifts. You celebrate with them. You grieve with them. You wait for them to come around. You forgive them. You may have to be on standby over financial matters too. You stay by their side without flinching even when the roof comes crashing down. You are "just like family." "You are not eating well enough; look at your flesh hanging on your bones" is also family. "Shall I look around for a suitable boy. Why are you not married yet?": there goes the family. They don't stop at "When are you going to give us a niece or a nephew?" It is perfectly natural for family to advise "Should you not be looking at open heart meditation?" There is free flowing counselling on investments, good diet, social protocol, extended family gossip, comparisons, judgements, validations, and repetitive jokes! A family has each other's backs. A family never gives up on you. A family loves you even though they may be struggling to like you. A family is primarily of the female gender! A family is also very exhausted. A family needs two weeks of sleep! And compassion fatigue is politically incorrect.

60

The Anglo-Indian

Have you had a childhood charmed by the presence of Anglo-Indians close by? Did you have a Gillian or a Deborah or a David in the neighbourhood? You were in awe of their lifestyle, which was very different from your saree and parantha and kerosene stove surroundings back in the 1970s. They frequently spoke of an uncle in Australia who got them a spinach eating, blue-eyed, golden mopped doll. David played with a wooden train and track set complete with carriages and an engine. The Woodman family lived in a huge bungalow atop a little hill. They drove in a light green Morris Oxford car, and their home smelt of fresh bakes. Sourdough bread! The wooden meat and tin pie safes caught your imagination completely. You marvelled at the homemade ginger wine they served in goblets on lace covered trays. At the Cantonment club, they did the close dance, often jiving to live music, moving gracefully on the polished, wooden floor. Their father wore a white shirt over khaki trousers. His moustache wagged under the sola topee. You visited their home in a state of awe-inspired shyness. One particular meal that included pumpkin soup, caramel custard, pork mish mash, and beef rumble dumble never left your mind. Mrs. Woodman owned bookcases full of Agatha Christie murder mysteries and Mills and Boons romances. She also owned a silver, perfume scent atomizer. You loved her floral tea dresses and kitchen Hindi. She would often have the family run their fingers over the grand piano in the hall as they sang Edelweiss. Today, when you read of Britain's forgotten grandchildren and the dilemma of identity they face, you feel homesick for the David you never knew!

III

CHEERFUL PESSIMISM

61

The Dog

Have you had a dog paw your hand back to scratch her belly? She goes still when you resume. Her ears go flat against her head and the eyes roll. There is a presence, a person inside of that body. You sense it in her steadfast gaze, weighty and substantial. She sees you. No words are exchanged, but the silence connects. You pull her close and engulf her in your arms. She rests her head deliberately on your shoulder. You let her be, then withdraw, presuming you are done with the day's dose. Just as you raise yourself on the knee, she pulls you back, and presses those ears again. She beseeches. You are getting late for something important on your schedule. You lope off with a slight shake of the head, and you miss seeing the forlorn look in those transparent eyes. Of course, you love the dog! She prances in with your socks in her mouth, daring you to chase her and snatch it back. But you are too tired after a day's work. She barks hopefully a few times then drops the article dejectedly to go flop in the corner from where she fixes you with a gaze that does not blink. You call her a silly girl, a foolish pup, an idiot even, but she comes bounding to greet you on your return home the following day, her wet nose rubbing against your shins. At a painful time one day, when your heart is full and your spirits low, she tiptoes over to you, places a paw on your knee, and holds your gaze in complete companionship. And you think, "Oh my God, I simply have to become the person my dog thinks I am!"

62

The Brand

Have you been given the up and down ever? Perhaps you have treated someone else to the gaze. The eyes scan sideways, your glance sweeping the frame vertically and back down again. "Too fat! Terrific outfit. Oh my God, look at those nails. A bargain shopper!" In a matter of seconds, you sort, slot, and spit out the individual. They have not yet opened their mouths, but the packaging has spoken to you. The footwear shouts. The handbag whispers. The jewellery murmurs. The wristwatch gossips. And the glasses chuckle. Brands are the shorthand of sizing each other up. Who has the time to get to know you? Let's make a statement about ourselves. A Fabindia type, big *bindi* included. A lower end brand, the Hidesign's *Holi* kind. The premium Emporio league, Bottega Veneta sorts. Sarojini Nagar versus Lajpat Nagar type? Oh yes, your appearance talks about you. You value money. You prefer personal style and comfort over money. You live from a place of plenty. You exist in a place of fear. You are a shrinking violet. You are a sensational frangipani. You care what people think of you. You have no use for other people's opinions. You are a consume and throw kind. You like your stuff to last. You live within your means. You quite clearly overdraft on your credit card. You gear up like a moonwalker on a trip out of home, waist pouch for all the essentials in place. You carry it all, gum and cardamom and wet swipes in your bag. But in the final analysis, it is neither what you wear nor what you carry on you. It really is your energy, your speech, and your actions that make for your very own, personal brand!

63

The Landing

Have you approached landing in an aircraft only to have the machine pull away from the airport for an orbit? One moment you are in descent upon a glittering floor and the next you are dragging against gravity, the bright lights fading into tentative twinkles. Your heart sinks. "Ladies and gentlemen, there has been an incident on the runway, and we have instructions to go around. We will hold for another twenty-five minutes to final descent!" the captain comes on. You shut your eyes tight, wishing the uncertainty away. You were so looking forward to stepping out into fresh air from the confined cabin. "What if we run out of fuel? What if this Colombian pilot has misunderstood the Air Traffic Controller's English? What if we crash-land? I have not left any instructions over my emerald necklace!" You kick yourself out of this scary vein of thoughts and sit up deliberately. There is a fatigued sound to the engine hum. The cabin crew is stiff, strapped up, and non-committal; no help there. You stretch and swivel your neck. The sleep heavy nods and glazed eyes of fellow passengers are strangely comforting. "Oh my God, even if one person panics, there will be hell to pay and no place to run!" You dare to peer out the window. Ink dark. No snaking toy cars. No psychedelic life. "Ladies and gentlemen, we are going down. Excuse me, we are beginning our initial descent!" The cabin comes to startled attention. There are several bumps, and you get that giant wheel, plummeting sensation in the groin. For a split second, the aircraft seems to stall, and your mouth goes dry. Then there is a wiggle waggle and the runaway thunders up at you. "Will this machine stop in time? Is there enough runway?" You brace yourself and grip the arms. Minutes later, you emerge onto the steps with the other pale, shaken passengers…all wanting their Moms!

64

The Snorer

Have you had trouble coming to terms with your snoring? You don't believe you snore at all. Tiny, delicate little snorelets perhaps but full-fledged, audio wonders, delivered at varying rhythm and pitch? Not a chance. Even when your partner records your somnolent orchestra one night and confronts you with evidence at dawn, you humour her with utter disbelief. "This only happens when I am tired and have had a drink or two!" is your defence. Oh, but do you snore?! You rip the peaceful night with rasps and rumbles; there are some frightening rhapsodies in your repertoire. Whissssk, wheeeedle, and wonk goes one. Seesee, saaiin, siimmmmm…goes another! Hurrramph hurrrrrrrr pheeeeen phrunk…you go! Obstructive sleep apnoea (OSA) is the medical term. The trumpeting and whistling originating due to an obstruction of air movement during breathing while sleeping. There is no conclusive cure for snoring. Lifestyle changes are recommended, and there are remedies such as orthopaedic pillows, nasal clips, dental splints, and even surgery in some cases. But these have to begin with an acknowledgement! How do you get a snorer to see and hear himself? He doesn't even know he is close to being smothered. Who hasn't cringed upon hearing a strangled gargle rising from the seats in a suspense-ridden movie hall? Or the rise of a tentative banshee wail in a library lecture? Or the anxious moments between the snorts from the form lying prone besides you at night, waiting for the nasal passage to strike again! And how in the slumbering world does the one who snore always manage to go to sleep first? But, of course, women snore too.

65

The Day

Have you had trouble explaining your day away? "What did you do today?" the question can stump you. Nothing comes to mind. You unpacked the new washing machine and read the instruction manual. Is it worth mentioning at all, you wonder! You sorted out and segregated some clothes. What a mundane chore! You made a couple of follow up phone calls on the TV repair, the refrigerator servicing, and some welcome and goodbye conversations. You also worked your social scene on WhatsApp. Would you consider any of it mention-worthy? Then there was the mango crop from the backyard. You had the fruit washed and cooked into a delicious jam. Now that is creative! It made you feel good; there was a sense of accomplishment. Supervision of the laundry, clearing of cobwebs, tracking the pantry stock, balancing kitchen accounts, watching some TV, a short nap may be, and waiting for the family members to come home. You may have done some online shopping and composed an email or two. There were the meals to keep track of and the dog's visit to the vet. You also carried out the routine airport and railway station runs. You are caught in a revolving door lady! You are after all, a homemaker. By choice? The world's most crucial but least lauded portfolio. And don't worry if the days seem to go slow because your years will go insanely fast!

66

The Cacophony

Have you had a sneaky feeling no one understands you? You could be right. It is because no one is really listening to each other anymore. So much has changed! There was a time when people kept a stiff upper lip. They believed their actions would speak for them. No more! We are in an age of libidinous communication. There is an unrestrained outpouring of views, perceptions, opinions, and feelings! We are all nodding our heads in apparent understanding and baring our teeth in grim politeness, but we are also frowning at the speaker's slow speech. His first intake of breath and we move in surgically with our own monologue. Watch a pair walking together in the park. The decibel levels are high but their sounds neither connect nor communicate. While one is spewing her spiel, the other is busy working in her mind on what she wants to say. The intent is not to understand but to reply! Interruptions are rampant and endemic. We begin politely enough: "I am sorry for interrupting...," and then we go right ahead and barge in. Context, content, co-empathy...it is all out of the window. We are just talking! At and around and beyond each other. Conversations cannot happen in the absence of listening. And most times, that is all people need for help, an ear that will pay them the ultimate human respect of attention. We really should occasionally use the golden chance to just shut up and listen.

67

The Slowing

Have you experienced several heart stopping moments at the growing signs of ageing in your parents? It begins with the feathery crisscross on the smooth hands that once wielded the rolling pin with energy and elan. You watch the gradual gnarling in disbelief. The clear forehead your Mum traced a bindi on goes as does her lovely dark plait. Dad is no longer as ramrod straight. People who once looked upon him with near awe now bear an indulgent smile as though to humour. Mum tells you how the cataract surgeon smiled when she asked for the best quality lens he could offer. Your heart twists and turns to see your life's heroes slowing down. The shoulders that carried you once stoop now. The eyes that embroidered and sewed for you, peer at your departing figure through a teary cloud. You realize with a never before intensity how they put you first above their own needs and comforts and desires always. They still do. Patient and silent, they remain in a standby mode besides you, ready with gifts and wisdom and prayers and cheer. They created wealth, remained committed to the generation before and after them, and valued their self-reliance and continue their industrious, productive, Spartan, and sustainable living to this day. Their actions and choices and decisions were dictated by a certain perception of the 'family good'. You want to emulate them. You marvel at their emotional resilience, physical stamina, and their capacity for giving. You wonder if you will ever match up to them. Then one day, as you sit with them under a bright garden umbrella on the front lawns of the beautiful home your dad built, your eyes boring into their wrinkles, Dad booms, "Old? Who, me? Never." And then, "Haven't you heard of Bernard Baruch? He said: Old age is always ten years older than I am!"

68

The Punjabi

Have you ever had your rose-tinted spectacles yanked off with force and finality? It leaves the eyes gritty with grief. The disappointment comes with an acute sense of helplessness. You were proud to have been born a Punjabi for one, almost chauvinistic at how your world showed two fingers to itself in rhythm to Bhangra beats! "It is a privilege to be born a Sikh," you were raised to believe. Punjabiyat flourished all around you, in Bollywood, JK Rowling's *Casual Vacancy*, and the ubiquitous pan-Indian salwar kameez. Along came *Udta Punjab*, erasing memories of the green and white revolutions with one jarring stroke. On a visit home, you meet the country cousins, marvelling at how far you have come from where you began. Their tight group dynamics, their sharp awareness of their environment, their measured tones come across as the bearings of a community under attack. Their analytical, almost clinical despair is strangely exhilarating…surely the only way out now is up. The landowners have mortgaged their fragmented holdings in lieu of Fortuners and Audis. The young have handed themselves over to synthetic drugs. The inherent Punjabi ego will not allow them the dignity of labour at home in the intensely class-ridden society. Regular jobs do not pay enough to support an above average lifestyle. Business is at the mercy of the government's menopausal policies. What is left to do is to marry an NRI citizen and flee the country to the anonymity that will permit them to live like the Punjabis are meant to live…in a state of perpetual celebration.

69

The Control

Have you ever been called out on your concern? You are concerned at your children coming home late. You are concerned at the amount of alcohol the adult consumes. Your concern is over their cigarette smoking. You concern yourself with their personal affairs…of the head and heart. Your middle name is concern. You cannot help concerning yourself with how your loved ones look and how much they weigh and just how dry their hair is and what in the world is happening to their skin? You are pretty concerned at their lack of sleep. Their oversleeping causes you concern too. You have a miniscule faith in their instinct for self-preservation. In fact, you fancy yourself as their saviour and moral compass. But for you, they would be long dead and done for. It is only your fretful worry and obsessive concern that keeps them out of harm's way. "Have you checked in online? Are you carrying enough money? Is your telephone charged? Do you have enough change on you? Has the worst-case scenario been visualized and rehearsed? Is there an alternate number I can call? Only in case of an emergency, you bet! Make sure to update us regularly. Keep us in the loop. We will be tracking you on the flight status and on Google Map. Inform us upon reaching. Are you carrying your first-aid box? You should carry some sandwiches too, just in case. How about a poncho for the rain? You really should use a dryer on that hair; you will catch a cold. Do you have that Uber app? Well, call one. Work backwards from the flight departure." Our anxiety for ourselves, our pet agenda of teaching our kids life's little lessons, our deepest desire to be seen as a great parent, our very real fear of having to share the consequences of poor choices, and our desperation to see our children flourish in our lifetime…these sentiments are playing havoc into our relationship with our young for whom we would otherwise throw ourselves in front of a breakneck truck. Could the control be pointing the wrong way?

70

The Icing

Have you wondered why perfectly great cakes feel the pressure to cover themselves up with frost and cream and butter and icing? Gross. Has anyone researched why and where this wasteful trend began? Icing tastes awful; there is just foam and grainy goo you shovel around in your screwed up mouth uselessly. You finally force yourself to swallow the frothy mass, eyes half shut with distaste. Then you need a napkin, even fingers to pluck the corners of the lips, free of the pretentious mess. There remain the baubles to deal with. Floral works of art, all leafy and scallopy. Glazed, brittle, melting…the garnish mostly goes in the dustbin. In fact, even when the cake wedges are doing the rounds in a platter, there is frantic attempt to scrape free a slice. You try and spoon out the cake bread, leaving thick layers of buttercream behind. There is nothing messier than a used, iced cake plate! It doesn't matter what the flavour is. Oh, it looks incredible, yes, but is it food at all? There is colouring and a sickly sweetness. And what amazing pastel shades to the slop that will only be artfully dodged around. Cakes really should remain naked, in the buff and in all their spongy, light feathery, nutritious, flavoured goodness. And those who pile perfectly yummy cupcakes with swirls of slosh will have to answer in heaven. And who said that the synthetic, syrupy, leathery cherry is the icing on the cake?

71

The Way

Have you carried a burden all your life over not having lived as you deserved to because someone or the other kept coming in the way? Your parents influenced your shape and size and colour with their genes. They gave you allergies, a pear-shaped bottom, and thick ankles. In senior school, you were powerless to exercise your choice of career. Born in India, you were decreed by the *shastras* to take coaching for admission to the country's elite professional schools. But you were young! Rebellion and experimenting were a given. Moreover, no one really put their foot down. "Aunty! I enjoy a smoke occasionally, and I am honest about it. My parents don't know because they never asked. If they did, I would admit to the habit." People. Others. Authoritative figures. They slowed you down on your path to a dazzling present and a brilliant future. There came the special other, the honey, the sweetie, the babe soon. They brought along with them their tear-jerking drama, bogging you down with their 'now hot now cold' emotional blackmail. You also knew a conspiracy when you saw one. You were not an educated, well read, abundantly provisioned youth for nothing. The UN crushed your idealism with their impotent fluff. That North Korean maniac proved you were right in your 'neither black nor white' views. Modi stood in your way of transforming India with your liberal altruism. The consumerism, corruption, communism-ridden planet held you back by sheer force of gravity, or you would have long escaped into the galaxy, blazing a trail of defiant immortality. There was always a teacher's pet, a boss's apple-polisher, an unfair superior, an abusive parent/ partner, a short-sighted policy, an inefficient domestic staff, a crumbling infrastructure, bad timing, some harsh weather, and more, holding you back. Of course, some people in life really are dealt lemons, but you on Facebook? It is you. And it is me. We really need to get out of our own way!

The Boys

This year again, the top spots in the X and XII national board exams have gone to the girls. There is a steadily growing social refrain that the female gender is more sincere and hardworking. Is this a myth, one wonders? Or is it a reality? Perhaps, it is part of both. Perhaps, the girls have always had to overcompensate and over-deliver while the boys are only now facing comparison in a newly shared space with them. It could also be the first spring of the girl-friendly season, the honeymoon so to speak of newly opened, smooth surfaced gender highways, facilitated by supportive parents, civil society, and "*Beti bachao, beti padao*" and "*Sukanya samridhi*" governance. The female sex definitely seems to have gotten a foot inside the gates to personal salvation, and more skylights keep opening up for them. Even the armed forces are throwing open their combat roles to women. But where are the boys amidst all this song and dance over girl empowerment? There is a school of thought that claims that boys are being academically neglected and emotionally persecuted by teachers whose training, style, and temperament favour girls. How then are the boys coping? Do they feel trapped in strictly defined gender roles? Are they confused as to the expectations from them? Do they feel anger at the strident feminism around them? Are they threatened by the pro-girl air they now have to breathe? Does it scare them to see patriarchy under attack and the consequent challenge to male authority? It is being claimed by some that the male reaction is taking the shape of young men refusing to grow up. They fail to launch, parking in front of the TV, holding ambition and productivity at bay. They spend their time watching violent video games. They are dropping out of colleges and chilling in their floaters and bermudas. They are returning home from life outside to live off their parents, resisting the responsibility of maintaining independent units and raising their own families. What schools and parents and the media can do is cultivate cross-gender sympathy and avoid comparison altogether. There are unique challenges both the genders are struggling with today. And women issues are no longer just about women; they are central to all humans. Look how they are affecting the boys!

95

73

The Toilet

Have you entered an aircraft toilet in a state of personal emergency only to recoil in horror at the mayhem inside? You swivel your neck around and glare at the retreating back of the earlier occupant, boring laser beams of frustration at the shrinking figure. He knows and is ashamed of his act of omission! What is it with us Indians and toilet etiquette? Is it that we begin to feel invisible in our crushing numbers? There are so many of us; who is going to notice? One more toilet roll yanked to the floor doesn't count. Another seat soiled; there are so many happening all over the place. There is such a cumulative fatigue of numbers that our antenna of consideration has jammed up. There is respect only for the friends and family, even acquaintances, but strangers? They are threats to your existence, contenders for scant resources. If you could, you would wish them out of existence. You back out of the narrow and defiled space now, scowling at your black thoughts. You let the brave-heart breathing down your neck take the muck on inside the loo as you squeeze past the passenger bulges and seek refuge in your seat, seething with an impotent rage at your Indianness. Your inner monologue rages, "The airlines should conduct toilet etiquette sessions for users. Many first-time travellers may not know of the sensor operations. There are these globetrotting groups banging and twisting and breaking handwash dispensers and sensitive taps in European washrooms. Who, in India, would dream of a foot pedal control for the water faucet? Indians have such a poor international image for hygiene; where do we begin? The country smells of piss. What to do? Where to go?" On your way out to the arrival terminal, you enter the bus from the aircraft in the claustrophobic heat and pull back in horror all over again. High and tight on the inflight beverages, a fellow countryman has spilled his guts on the bus floor. What's our excuse this time?

The Sleep

Have you been alarmed at how little sleep people appear to get these days? The entire global village seems wide awake round the clock; it is not just the night-shift people. Social media begins to ping and buzz with a vengeance as darkness falls. The graveyard workforce swings by friendly places to chill after the night's job is done. No one bats as much as an eyelid. People think nothing of texting and WhatsApping at what were until recently considered impolite hours of the day. What is going on? Have we as a species metamorphosed into these all-time, all-weather creatures? Or are we stuck in an artificial time construct that is playing havoc into our system? After dinner is when multitudes of people log back into their online accounts. In fact, nobody seems to be logging out anymore. Our smartphones keep us in a constant state of high. Our bodies may appear at rest towards the wee hours, but our thoughts and ideas and emotions are flapping and fretting and fuming. More people are pro-actively engaged with each other at night than ever before. It is scary that these very same chattering insomniacs then strike out the following day to fly planes and perform surgeries and fight court cases and cook food. Is there any wonder then that people snap at each other or knock each other down or just plain lose their marbles? Sleep apnoea! It is running rampant as per reports in our country. We wake up several times during the night, we don't exercise, we go to sleep late, and consume heavy meals. Dinner is often preceded by "large" and "small" affairs. The young add to their health deficit in the lethal belief that their youth can handle sleep deprivation. Our coffee incorporation is faulty moreover. Unlike its late arrival in our drawing rooms after the meal, it comes after an early supper in healthier societies. Welcome, therefore, to the exponentially growing sleep therapy market. Loosen them purse strings now, will ya, for something that was free as air and water and laughter until now.

The Bargain

Have you gloated over a smart deal you got yourself? The whole world gets to know about your adroit negotiation. You feel redeemed. You got more for less. You did not let the other get the better of you. You stopped short of being taken for a ride. You did not end up the sucker. You were shrewd. Life is a mean dog-eats-dog tenure. And you are the meaner canine! The world is out to get you. No way you are letting that happen. You will be darned if you let any idiot pull the wool over your eyes. You are a bargain ninja! You get the most out of what life hands you. You anticipate. You cover your tail. You keep your situational awareness honed. You have seen life up and close. You know what human nature is all about. The other guy better not be messing with you. Don't they know how hard you work and with such integrity! Can they not see how positive you are? Surely it beams out of your ears, the good will that you bear others. You have not hurt as much as a fly all your life. The tiny white lies were just to spare others unnecessary hurt. You are a good, kind, fair, and genuine human, a premium sample of the Homo sapiens. Why is *panditji* shouting above the crowds now? "A graha shanti homam with 10,000 recitals and aarti will cost 16,000 rupees, madam!" Does he not know you are a careful spender? You do a quick mental calculation. "God is everywhere! And I am a good human being. I can pass this one." On your way out of the temple to the car parking, your hand creeps up reflexively to your suddenly burning right ear. The nine stone gold stud is missing! You have always taken extra care to keep the screws nice and tight! It cost you 49,700 rupees for the pair.

76

The Nameless

Have you felt that humid, bone-weary fatigue at the sheer numbers pressing into you in public spaces around our country? The crowds grab you by the throat. You edge one way and then the other. Someone's bag pokes you at completely unexpected angles. A body part is sure to brush you. Your personal space is only in your mind. In real time, people are upon and over and under and around you. There is the palpable stench of sapped resignation. Everywhere you go, there are rosters and lines and token numbers. And people do await their turn in most cases. Are they too enervated to rage at the time it takes their turn to come? Or is it the stoic heroism of the ordinary? A humdrum, predictable constancy. You note the namelessness in those masses. You are struck by the limited resources evident in their bearings. You can't help but marvel at their unflinching visages. They merely shrink and curl in the face of authority, no protest. They accept their place in the scheme of things. They do not demand anything. They go about the business of waiting, expressionless and inscrutable. Look around India's public spaces. There are two sisters bound in a companionable silence. A young man struggles with his grandfather's wheelchair. The babes nuzzle into maternal necks. You watch a father wait patiently as his wife digs out reference papers from her cloth bag. These are the swathes of India's silent citizenry. They skimp and save and sacrifice and stay the course. In the hope of something better? Or because, what else is there to do?

77

The Legacy

Have some of your long-held desires been lost to time and chance? Perhaps you were going to become a world-famous journalist. There may have been a teenage crush you had to relinquish to parental wisdom. Did you fancy yourself living in a red tiled, white picket fenced little cottage instead of the multi-storeyed apartment you now inhabit? There was a pair of sun glasses, a handbag, a perfume, or a particular car that you fancied. You were going to be rich and famous in your mid-twenties. There were charming places awaiting your footfall. You could have been an evolved soul, a bestselling novelist, a scientific inventor, a master artist, a maestro, a virtuoso! What happened to that house on the beach and the three loping dogs? You were going to have that perfect ten-on-ten partner. Your kids would not know a better parent. You had your notions, your convictions, and your passions. Then life happened, and your parents passed on the adult mantle to you. You got on with it pretty much with verve and some elan. The bridge you straddle today has a lot of water flowing under it. You have lived well. You have made your family proud. You have lifted the little world around you with your sterling example. Professional success, family affection, physical comfort, opportunities for growth…you have it all. But your children give you that look you know all too well: "Hey, you guys are such safe bores. You gave up too much. You did not live enough. You are too scared. You work too hard. You don't have enough fun. I'm going to be so different!"

The Stow

Have you stowed away small sachets of ketchup and those tiny, adorable, vacuum-packed cubes of butter in your travel bag ever? And how about the shampoo, conditioner, body lotion packs they lay out in hotel baths? Did you ever sneak in a headphone from the on-flight entertainment, thinking it would come in handy with the laptop or the smartphone at home? It is a national fetish. We find it impossible to throw away perfectly good articles. No one really knows what happens to the stuff. Where do all the unopened bread buns go for one, all those plump bags from the half-finished meal trays? The salt and pepper and sugar strips? Are they recycled, or does some of the host staff put it to use? Such apparent wastage in a five-star hotel is a whole another level. The tiny jars of fruit preserves and syrups and Nutella, those delicious mini mounds of butter in gold foils, the aromatic teabags, the welcome chocolates…they are all good for multiple uses, and it is tempting not to think "waste," but there you go. Napkins, face towels, conference candy, note pads, extra pens…we stow them all. Think temporary identity cards, bite-sized snack packs, small juice cartons, and plastic spoons and cups and stirrers…a true-blue Indian bag will have it all. In a nation of abundant poverty, malnutrition, and food insecurity, there is no way we are returning a bottle of wine with the tiniest of dregs. We will stow them all, inside the stomach and outside, the bows and the ribbons and the envelopes and the rubber bands. Give us this day, our daily stow!

79

The Race

Have you suffered politically incorrect feelings in the company of Indians abroad? You waddle around in your brown ethnicity, all of you, not in the best of fitness states and quite generously proportioned in the lower extremities. The average of you all is neither petite nor lofty. You look and behave like the endangered sparrows as against the proud peacocks. Of course, there is a disarming friendliness in your eyes. You are quite economical in occupying space too. You all are not demanding, moreover. There is an endearing shyness to your smiles by all means, but you are no match for the prototypes that stride around you. You look at those magnificent, cream-coloured races with their aqua/azure eyes and golden crowns. They have goddess frames, long and lithe. Even the fingers are tapering and the toes slender. You steal a glance again to make sure the noses are aquiline and the eyes in bloom. These living, breathing, gorgeous men and women resemble the resplendent sculptors in some of Europe's heritage museums. Perfect proportions, exercised limbs, and squeaky-clean skins. You shudder at the thought of the sub-replacement fertility of some of these world's most good-looking nationalities. Who is conserving this gene bank of human beauty? There are political, social, and economic factors behind long term population decline, yes, but the sense of loss is over the human attractiveness at stake. Is this racism? Of the skin-deep kind?

The Homemaker

Have you noticed the utter lack of stories about you? You! An educated, sub-upper middle class, reasonably well-travelled, well-read, articulate gentle-woman. You play by the rules, you live within your means, your heart beats for the disadvantaged, you know your wines and cheeses somewhat, and there sits the tiniest crinkle on your nose at the Indian circus. You ought to be hailed as the quintessential heroine, but no one writes about you. The slums get coverage, as do the fancy chateaus of the rich and famous. The dons and rapists guzzle reams of newsprint, and celebrities walk away with their bestsellers, but you are too mundane to cause any literary ripple. The backwaters of Kerala get written about, as do the lofty peaks around the Pangong Tso, but your humdrum little urban home does not hold a writer's imagination. Only the advertisers seem to love you. For the rest of them, you are invisible. You have no nuisance value. You represent nothing but a bland conformity. All you have done is work hard at a mediocre job, get married, produce kids, and be a general bore. The most exciting thing you have probably ever done is attend your child's graduation. You don't spend much on yourself, you keep your jewellery in the locker, you absorb family crisis, you often exhale deeply and call out to the almighty in your prayers. You are a receptacle for your child's disappointments with life; you humour their ribbing; you swallow the lump in your throat at their occasional insensitivity. You are the anchor and the motor of your unit. You know, don't you, that the family and the world think you have not done much with your life. But you also ought to know that civilizations are built upon the foundation of happy and functional homes and you…you incredibly giving creature…you nudging, cajoling, nagging little voice… you annoying nosy meddler…you ambitious pusher…you interfering moral compass…you are that homemaker. And you just got written about!

81

The Souvenir

Have you smiled thinly at a perfume bottle being pushed at you by an overseas relative? Your mind's eye recognizes the name vaguely. It looks half decent, but a vicious voice goes beeping in your head: "Sale item… they have so many of those abroad!" The imported gifts come in bulk. Nail enamels, the shades entirely unsuitable for brown skins. Deodorants, in multiples, leaving you wondering if there is a message there! Chocolates, ranging in the minty to the vitiligo condition. There are too many of those, but you don't have the heart to give them away to someone else so they end up dry and crusty and useless in the refrigerator. And who has not tried on the faintly aromatic, second-hand garments, one after another, only to accept some out of sheer exhaustion. "This should be fine!" you express a weak gratitude. Souvenirs from other nations are indeed, hard-work. A lot of calculation, estimation, conversion, and apprehension is involved. "Could this puny tray be available back in those arty stores at the Khan Market?" And then, "These pink crystal goblets are a replica of the green ones I bought in Ahmedabad!" Everything seems to be available everywhere. There does not seem any authentic local product visible anymore. There is this vast, uninspiring, universally Chinese gift fill. Ah yes, there are the magical pain balms and the Tylenol! Surely the foreign drugs are better quality, but who would be kicked at pharmaceutical gifts? So, what are the two, next best things to do? Share your experience with foreign coins for one! And should your pocket be deeper, come back home, go online, and order all kinds of treasures from travels you did not know, were authentic and representative of their regions! Jam jars from Alsace, Papaw ointment from Australia, Icelandic sheepskin, Bushwick candles, Turkish towels, Swiss Murray's cheese and Maggi Hot and Sweet sauce from India.

82

The Acceptance

Have you gotten the impression that the rate of acceptance has crash-landed over just one generation? Not the college acceptance kind but that too! No one around anyone seems able to accept the other fully, barring Mum, if one is lucky! Someone in your radius is forever trying to fix you. A parent or a spouse or a sibling, even a well-meaning friend. Fixing from teachers and trainers and bosses and sellers is acceptable, it is even expected, but those we do the honour of associating with on emotional terms, their acceptance could end up being a matter of life and death! There is nothing costlier and dearer than the gift of free acceptance. It frees your body cells to get on with the task of being; it lifts your spirit and lets it rise with capacity-full lungs. It gives your mind the space to dream and create and forge. Hell, it gives you permission to live! But in most cases, what happens is that you are never able to fit someone else's ideal notion of you. You are either overweight or not eating enough. You are either too blunt or a bit of a people pleaser. You are either too loud or too reticent. You are either unhygienic or obsessively clean. You need to exercise. You need to be more careful with money. You do not plan investments enough. Your anger management in traffic needs work. You let your friends take advantage of you. You don't communicate enough. You need to be fixed, put right, corrected, altered. Human lives are about self-constitution and reflection in the daily hubbub of life and achieving your own degree of excellence at your own pace. What then, does the itch to fix, say about our inner wounds of self-loathing and judgement? Maybe, we ought to fix that first.

83

The Memory

Have you heard a note in the middle of nowhere and had a heart-stopping flash of a memory? A long-forgotten face. A half-remembered moment. A foggy recollection of a pleasant evening. A twinge almost at the images. Where could those people be? Whatever happened to them? The Facebook thought strikes, but you dismiss it at birth. Some things are best left alone. Guarded and safe in their careful, bubble wraps in the mind and heart. There is the faintest of fears that should you pinch so much as a bubble, a molten lava might ensue. It is a strange sentiment. Those people exist inside of you but beyond an acknowledgement. You even have a simmering fondness for them, but it is frozen. They pop into your mind's eye at odd times, but you look through that once familiar collage. They are trailers of what might have been! Of what ought not to have been. It is human to wonder "What if?" But you move on with strength. A call was taken. A decision made. The fork was resolved. Some associations are even more fleeting. A half-hour walk to the doctor's and back. An evening spent together in the company of a big crowd. A conversation with a fellow passenger on a flight. And it leaves a forever impact on you. You never meet them again. And they probably have no clue your heart clicked a selfie of them! With time, the recall takes on sepia tones, in years, only to remain as a feeling perhaps; you forget the specifics, even imagine some. And then you tell yourself, "Hey, you are a memory too! To them. Best hope then, that you be a faint fragrance than a sharp grit behind their eyeballs."

The Scare

Have you been asked by a European of Indian origin, "Should these people be scared of China and India?" You take your time to respond. You are, after all, a self-effacing product of a non-violent civilization. While you are still composing an automatically reassuring apology in your head, your voice box breaks out independently. "Yes." The desi foreigner looks surprised. "Really? But is Modi any good? What about his Hindutva agenda?" he asks hopefully, perhaps trying to validate the decision to live abroad he made thirty years ago. You pause, then clear your throat. Patriotism is a fool's opium; you have intellectualised that fact from all your readings. There are things you both hate and love about your motherland. You loathe the filth and are ashamed of the dehumanizing poverty, but you also adore the disarming, even suicidal openness of the people. You abhor the self-serving politics and its associated shenanigans, but take pride in the country's survival as a singularly diverse nation. There is disease, there are rapes, and rule is a speck of lint on the sleeve, but through some strange algorithm, India survives. In fact, it flourishes. There has been no internal coup. Our brand of dictatorship looks like the present arrangement. No foreign power has stepped on our innards and rendered us ghostly. The rickshaw driver still pontificates on the power equations of the ruling family. The sweeper continues to hum K L Saigal's songs. The beggars and homeless survive on religious charity. The middle class struggles to keep its mask of honour in place but is also the driving force behind the country's holding economy. The Indo-European is looking at your smart floral shirt. "Did you buy this in Paris?" he wants to know. He is pleasantly surprised to learn it was sourced back home. "Is there reason to fear India?" he repeats. You know the truth. India has a long way to go. The level of openness to change, that degree of ambition and cutting-edge innovation needed to hit the big league is some way coming. But your voice is firmer this time when you say, "Go, figure!"

85

The Departure

Have you met people who can't bring themselves to leave home? They flit around their room agitatedly, gathering themselves up, but the exit does not happen. They are almost at the front door when they suddenly remember the bottle of water. "I should read the newspapers. Let me carry some reading material. Oh, the drive is long; where is that neck pillow of mine? I had downloaded some nice music. There has been no time. This drive would be perfect. There are clouds overhead; better carry an umbrella along. Have I switched off all the lights? I should pop some mouth freshener. One final trip to the washroom. Where is my man Friday? Some last-minute instructions." They do round off their one-way pontification to the Jeeves and slide into the car eventually. But barely out of the front gate and they have scrambled back into the house. They forgot their medicinal lotion! There was also some alteration work they could carry along; the tailor happened to be on the way. Now where did they keep their third phone? Tripping over a step, dropping an article or so, their four limbs trying to get to eight spots, they sail forth again with renewed resolve. "The food! How could I have forgotten the fruit? Has the cook stuck toothpicks on the lid? It can be so messy to munch on the whole apple." Their window of productive time is rapidly closing in the meanwhile. There is some homework to catch up with on return home too. They decide to take the plunge. An hour, not more, out in the dust and grime and they are back to their clean and cosy base. "I think I will take a short nap!" they declare to no one in particular.

The Singer

Have you stared into space at a gathering as a toneless song wrings itself out of an Indian throat at one of those innumerable parties where the fallback time filler is always, "Chalo! Let's have someone sing?" After much mock demurring, someone is sure to oblige. Beware, the world! Songs are forever rolling off the tips of Indian tongues. We are all a grand pool of undiscovered vocal talent. Watch us deliver. If it is a woman singing, she contracts, tilts her head to one side, and renders the song in a scale several notches too high. The male puffs out, fixes his gaze at a point on the floor, and then takes a break to scan the room a bit sheepishly. The melody drags on, rising and falling at excruciating scales; your body gets more and more rigid. You watch the singer open-mouthed, marvelling at that soulful "India's got talent" look on the face. "Please forgive us our sins, respected Rafi sahab and Lataji," you chant feverishly in your head. The voice is stretched thin now, teetering at the edge of the highest note, and the room forgets to breathe. A community muscle spasm begins. People shut their eyes, willing the singer to sail over, but the voice crashes short, landing shaky and spluttering. We can tell a bad note from a mile! And we are non-discriminatory with regards to the occasion and choice of song. We sing them all. Song of pathos at a wedding anniversary. Song of joy at a farewell function. The important thing is to sing. And shastriya sangeet came to us as early as the twelfth century CE! So, we know, you see.

87

The Pose

Have you noticed how we all freeze into sultry poses for the exclusive benefit of the camera? Something happens to our bodies. It is not conscious. Certainly not! It is all those images in the air that we breathe. The eyebrows reach up, just so. You widen those eyes and fix that lens with a seductive stare, well almost. Whoosh! That is the stomach going in. The knee bends, just the slightest. Ah, now that tightens the fabric around the thigh, giving it a slim silhouette. Your chest out, just a teeny bit, not too much please…that would be overt. But a gentle thrust gives your image some body; these pictures are going to be uploaded on some forum or the other after all, you know that. Tilt the pretty chin the slightest bit. And finally, the finishing touch: hand on the hip! Over the one not tucked behind a handbag or another body, in an attempt to portray svelte. Bare the pearlies at long last. Cheese. The lips split, fighting a pout that is descending automatically. The hair! Wait, wait, wait. Fluff it out, first this way, then that, or the pate will glower through the scanty scalp. Unknown to you, all this while, some candid photography has already taken place. The posing drill captured in frames! "That's alright; it is my own camera," you assure yourself, grabbing it back from the photographer. Some more time is spent on ruing the shaken images: cropping the good ones and filtering and deleting the duplicates. Hey, presto, the group photo gets uploaded. And you'll be darned if everyone isn't busy looking at themselves. They give you only a cursory look before going back to themselves in magnified bits. You shake your head and blink. Blink. And blink.

88

The Helper

Have you ever landed a helper who subsequently struck terror in your heart? They appeared harmless enough at the audition meet. The smile was a winning one, and the face wide-eyed. How were you to know they were partially deaf? They nodded vigorously to your searching questions. All had seemed fine. Now, well into your working partnership, you begin making nasty discoveries about the poker-faced one. You wonder how in the world organizations kept such loose cannons on payrolls. They seemed to stay and flourish, even intimidating the new inductees with their "We have been here forever" air. Take Shakuntala, for one. Shaku had been making hospital beds for close to thirty-five years. She sponged invalid patients, combed their hair, fetched them their meals, and pitched in with several other housekeeping chores. Her tasks were imprinted in her muscles, formidably automatic memories. She just flowed, unhindered by the cries of despair from her victims. If they asked her to buy them a cup of curd from the cafeteria at night, she would return triumphant carrying a soda as well. "But, no, you asked me to get this too!" While you would still be struggling to pull your fresh shirt down your torso, she would make a grab for the hooks and strap you up from behind. By force! She used sheer might on all the delicate hospital equipment. Even as you were frantically shooing her off the intravenous bottle, she would dive at the knob to turn it off. "Have you brushed? Shall I get you your breakfast? Why don't you let me add some butter to your *khichdi*? You will fall off the bed; let me raise the railings!" Good old, pushy, unmindful Shaku. You lie there, sore and throbbing, eyes darting at her flitting figure, waiting for her to strike. Then the matron comes and asks, "Ma'am, how do you find Shakuntala?" You want to beg for deliverance, but what comes out of the mouth is a tame reply, "Shaku? She is a sweet old soul!"

89

The Park

Have you lumbered into a garden, dragging mental cobwebs but come out feeling squeaky clean at the end of an hour? You are in plenty of company. Parks are like giant, organic vacuum cleaners. The green branches reach into the mind and dust out the worries. The mulchy flower beds are like Jacuzzis, pinching fatigue out of toxic human muscles. The wet breeze caresses clogged skins, brushing burning eyes and ringing ears. There, in the giant green spa is the integrity of effort, the brilliance of discipline, and the scent of hope. That jiggling midriff shall be sculpted. Those love handles will be chiselled. The heavy upper arms shall be carved clean yet. Race ceilings shall be crushed. Soaked in sweat, ear phones plugged and determination writ large on triumphant faces, men and women beat the earth. There is victory in getting out of bed and setting out in one's jogging shoes. There is a sense of accomplishment in stacking up an hour's worth of exercise. There is a lightness by osmosis from other people straining and pushing and expending. The yoga lot, the runners, the stretching gymnasts, the bhajan chanters, the charity doers, the colony group, the neighbourhood lads, the stray dog champions. "I avoid the concrete. Let's take the shortcut through the mangroves; that path is full of oxygen," the voices carry. "I just don't fit into my clothes anymore" floats by. And, "Have you any idea how lucky my cousin's daughter-in-law has been for their family?" Then, "Your visit home is due, alright? You absolutely must come over." There, on those dusty tracks and grassy lawns are friendships, fitness, self-love, and people we are destined to be. And for free!

The Non-vegetarian

Have you ever been annoyed at a vegetarian for being one, particularly when you are hosting them? The paneer people! Now, what novelty can you come up with for these difficult folks? If only they would go non-veg for that one meal. To find substitutes for chicken, mutton, and fish is a tall order; your hospitality seems lesser somehow. And horror of horrors, some of them keep off eggs too. Has anyone ever heard of a decent dessert without this miracle binder? To make an all-vegetarian pudding next, what a bother! The vegetarians, they spread unhappiness wherever they go. Their presence is a hostess's nightmare on Continental dinner tables in India. It is worse in Europe. No one understands the term there. What are you to conclude from this refrain: "Your husband is normal, and you are vegetarian! Him, he is normal, but you? You are vegetarian." The goat cheese salad you order comes topped with Boulettes de boeuf, beef cutlet in short. At your cry of dismay, the server whisks it away and returns the dish with two rich saucy depressions where the offending discs had nestled. Your heart cries as one, with the hordes of Indian travellers trawling the world on energy from French fries and lettuce and yoghurt. They grin and bear the barely concealed denial. "When did you turn vegetarian? What happened? Are you on a karmic retribution?" The armed forces handle these preferences like they negotiate all else…with ceremony. But gaffes happen. At one formal banquet, single roses were used to mark the vegetarian place settings. Thrilled to find a charming lady seated beside him, the General picked up his rose and made a presentation of it in a fit of chivalry. There was plenty of dance thereafter to go with the skilful music being played by the naval band.

IV

BEYOND ALL

The Expression

Have you ever said "I love you" to someone and waited? Silence ensues. A heart-stopping moment later, you cock your head, and an eyebrow goes up. Still nothing. Just as the steel begins to knock at your eyes, the object of your affection reaches out clumsily with a weak laugh. "Arey! I love you too, bhai." The moment passes; life resumes. But you are left with a nagging feeling. How come in some parts of the globe, these three words flow free as water? But back home, in India, they drag themselves around, soaked in a cocktail of confusion. They don't seem to sit easy on tongues that have, for centuries, defined love as committed and consistent action. A father loves with his unfailing provision and protection. A mother loves unconditionally by putting her family and home first. Children love by growing up in affirmative ways. Grandparents love by valuing and validating their grandchildren. What, therefore, is this need for a constant assertion and expression of love? And in all manners and mediums. Balloons. Confetti. Love pillows. The merchandising of a value that is impossible to structure and contain in three words. Eight characters and such a storm. The permutations do not stop. It is now "I love you, but I do not like you!" Well, you just had your toilet cleaned with your toothbrush. Can you love without liking? Can you like sans respect? Can you love but not respect? What say the Mensa of love?

92

The Giver

Have you got a box full of old shoes you no longer wear but expect to use someday? You trim and filter the pile regularly, but a sizable number find their way back in. Most are no longer the current style. Some are not the exact fit. A couple have seen better days. But they are all relatively unused and that qualifies them as indispensable yet. Who in their right mind gives away fresh-looking possessions? So, you sit on them until they go brittle with protest one day. The *Zari* work dullens, and the elastic begins to sag. It is only then that the courage to give away stirs inside of you. But like all other aspects of modern life, this sequence is changing. Gone are the days when the food close to putrefaction would be waved off to the domestic help. "Here, these are clothes you might want to use," saying this, your mom would hand over the pile of old clothes to her grateful maid. Your grandmother exchanged her used robes for steel utensils; nothing was given away. Your children now urge you constantly to donate not just your old new suits but also household effects. Perhaps there is that luxury now of surplus. It inspires the confidence to share. Co-working spaces are here to stay, for instance. The millennials are donating online as a part of curating their social selves. The writing is clear on the wall. It is no longer good enough to merely be compassionate. You have got to act. The word is tithing.

The Peacemaker

Have you been told you are too spread-out for anyone's comfort? Too adventurous. Too attention-seeking. Too hungry for validation. Too much of a bad example. Why are you not content with just learning the violin for one? Why add French to your list too. Isn't it enough to be running half marathons? Do you have to play golf as well? Sit in one place and be calm, woman. You crackle too much. You try too hard. You try! So, you try to take a cue and back off. The tune promptly changes! Shouldn't you be putting your time to better use? Learn something new all the time; it keeps ageing at bay. Your children and family respect you more if you assume charge of your own happiness. Engaging with your environment keeps you relevant and healthy. So, then you break momentum yet again to take stock. Men have their crosses to bear, oh yes, but there is a greater acceptance of their fundamental right to just be themselves. Think of your women friends. One is too pushy; another whines too much, quite an aunty. The third has been a terrible mother. Some are too permissive with their children while the rest too controlling. Too fat, too much hair, too jowly, too blingy. The most palatable a woman can be, is spiritual! For some reason, they are never enough. A lifetime of trying to fit in. Unending moments of keeping it together at great personal cost. Years of being a support, the driving force, always on emotional standby, called in when needed. And all on a dark fuel of guilt, self-doubt, control by proxy, and a dash of tentative optimism. Of course, you give your daughter wings, then hold her back by their tips. Fear for her safety and dignified survival blights your friendship with her. And you are going raging chaotic inside with nearly three fourths of your own gender insisting to you, "What is the big deal with women? We have always had it good. Look how the young girls are misusing today's women-friendly policies!" Hello, second sex! What have you made your peace with?

The Gap

Have you had delusions about yourself being progressive that got pricked like a giant hot-air balloon? You thought you had the pulse of modernity and thereby the most potent of guidance for your young. Now you sit and rub the grit out of your eyes, staring disbelievingly at the lay of the land that appears to have been trampled upon by typhoons, tsunamis, and hurricanes. What happened? You were brought up to trust people, doctors, and teachers in particular? Phenomena such as the commercialization of Medanta Healthcare and the Delhi Public School brands were not even glimmers of an idea back then. Business was far removed from education and healthcare. Your dad taught you to respect authority and professional competence. Those in power were supposed to have your best interest at heart. There were individual anomalies, but the system was inherently fair, just like in a Bollywood movie where the good eventually came on top. You shrink now in fear and horror at the sales targets outlined by corporates for the medical and the pedagogical community. You watch helplessly while your overeducated young struggle to build jobs that cannot be defined by degrees. Education was supposed to be the magic key to security and prosperity. How did we come to discount experience outside schools so summarily? You struggle with an innate fear of straying from the norm, the straight and narrow. Just when it is needed most desperately, you decide all inventiveness that is not nine-to-five is laziness. You really are out of depth here, trying to canvass religion as a last resort, passing it off as some kind of moral and spiritual anchor when the young see how it is at the heart of every major scandal and controversy. From your quivering parental perch of a monumental mess, you exclaim at the next generation not wanting to bring kids into this world. Over-controlling and protective, you perpetuate the fear that one wrong decision can mean the end of the world. But the leaves, thank heavens, will turn, and you know you will pass. Today's young will become tomorrow's parents in spite of you. Who is to say what their challenges will be? You pray that they will find the strength and wisdom and love you did at last count.

95

The Status Quo

Have you ever had trouble concentrating on one social acquaintance at a large gathering? They are saying something animated to you, but your eyes are busy scanning and panning the glittering crowd. "Who else do I know? Who do I need to acknowledge once? Are there friends I might miss out on?" you fret to yourself, mouthing distracted responses to the raconteur. Your exchange is punctuated by brisk nods at the fast-moving snacks. The waiters interrupt whatever little flow of thoughts you both have managed to build up. You voice a profound getaway line soon, "Excuse me, let me go around. Catch up with you again soon!" Your next social stop is as lame; you are again skimming the crowd. The human hum around you pings your radar occasionally. People inquire of each other's well-being, children, and post-retirement plans. There are several exclamations over the beautiful sarees and jewellery. The men talk shop. You flit and fan out farther, looking for one moment based on truth. With a few, there is a catalysis of mirth borne out of shared history and a priceless trust. For the rest, there is a gigantic parachute of safe subjects and good old ribbing, masking the real stuff seething underneath. More people come in. The vortex of exchange resumes, smiles aplenty, innumerable sweeping statements that do not expect to be challenged. No one loses, no one gains, everyone leaves intact for home. In the car though, you exchange some notes with the spouse to establish you were both heroes of the evening, having said the right things and danced the scripted, social choreography. Ah, a sigh of relief! Status quo reaffirmed and maintained.

96

The Hound

Have you killed your pet with kindness? She sits outside on the lawns in full view of the food chain, happily worrying her mutton bone. A sharp-eyed vulture swoops down at the unmindful mutt, menace writ large in her beady eyes. The dog ducks in terror, ears flattened back in fear, the white of her lovely eyes rolling. Her juicy bone bounces out of her slack mouth to settle at a distance, and she tries to grind herself into the ground. You are horror struck at her paralysis. Why won't she run? Why does she not growl back at the bird? Your parental switch kicks in, and you hoot at the sky in rage. You gather up the pet, snatch back her food, and huddle quickly into the safety of your home. "Switch on the AC and straighten her bed!" you direct your confused domestic help. The pet is still staring at you beseechingly, tears of mortification near the surface. Then she flops onto the rescued bone, her suicidal lack of self-defence all but forgotten. Silence ensues, punctuated by sounds of a delighted demolition. You watch her thoughtfully. Of course, you have done her a disservice by so domesticating her. She is no longer an instinctive animal. But she is precious and your teacher. You and I have to learn from her to simply be there for our loved ones. We need to, exactly like her, not say anything, not fix anything. Dear God, how does she let it be known that she is on our side and cares for us! This hound is the better human.

97

The Host

Have you ever been in the thick of spring cleaning only to be asked by your kid, "Is someone coming home?" The children wonder. Extrahard brasso and special food means guests are expected. The pretty linen elbows its way out of deep closet recesses. It is insane, the spit and polish that goes into hosting. The metal must reflect, the plants better shimmer, and the lawn be mowed afresh. There must be a shipshape turn to the air too, in the house. Monogrammed towels and fresh soap in the guest bathroom, phenyl balls on the drains, tea lights and aroma diffuser in place…the food preparation and presentation taken to a whole different league. What is with putting on a flawless show? Why can't we just relax over a casual, no stress, "we are like this only" meal? What compels regular folks to transform into obsessive, compulsive housekeepers at the mention of people coming home! It probably is a mix of several factors. One, the hostess's self-esteem is on the line here; her community judges her for her hosting bar. She is expected to keep a smart home and turn in a spectacular meal. Perhaps it is the subconscious tail end of our traditional conditioning that says, "A guest is akin to God." Somewhere we hold hospitality to be a reflection of our family, our home, our culture, even country at times. The modern dynamics of nuclear, no help, both-partners-working families may bring on panic and irritation at unexpected visitors, but we can be trusted for a long time yet to continue to be violently cheerful hosts. Or meet your entertaining commitments outside?!

98

The Words

Have you ever sat staring at a blank computer screen? You tap at the keyboard desultorily, then stab at the backspace key. A cup of steaming cardamom tea later, you are still at sea. The thoughts are fickle, and the words in a mood to tease. You dive and grab and stretch and fish, but the strings of sentiments elude you, circling your exasperated mind, just out of reach of your fingertips. You get up, step out, stretch your limbs, even splash water on your face, but the sentences stay stubbornly out of sight. You give up for the moment and step away. "Give them time to stew, those words," you tell yourself. And you get into the car to run some errands while the phrases are making up their minds. You have barely hit the first red light when the avalanche comes crashing all over you. There is a deluge of just the right ones. Fully formed ideas in neat stanzas, clicking neatly into your head, crying to be shared. You go on auto pilot, letting them take you hostage. They cover you. They fall off your lashes, tickle your nose, and go kissing those ears. You begin to drown in the lightening connections, in the cogent creative eruption. You know you have to stop right away and put down the piece descending upon you as though from thin air. You pull up, fumble into your bag for the Dictaphone, and switch on the microphone. The words quickly line up and sail into your growing piece of writing obediently. You feel potent, rich, able to fill up reams with your writing, but you switch off when the format has been met. Ah! That was a sweet spot you just hit. You sit back, feeling alive, feeling fortunate, a little bit drunk on your own words.

99

The Garb

Have you been hoarding some clothes long past their prime because the fabric is soft with age and you love the comfort of its smoothness against the skin? A night dress with a heavily smudged print. A very senior tee shirt with no pretences to appearance or form. A pair of frayed capris. Even an over-the-hill suit with knicks in the dupatta. You have set them aside during every cupboard sorting but snatched them back to your bosom just in time. They are your comfort gear. Your skin breathes in them, and they keep you free of annoying scratches. The regulations on care have long gone from the oversized labels. They are so inclusive as to have the size blanked out with wear. You worry your lip every time you pull them out; there is the tiniest bit of guilt at the shame associated with rags. But you shrug. At worst, some family member might chide, "What is that shabby wear you have on?" You might quickly have to jump out of them on occasions, demanding decorum. Some snide suggestions may be thrown your way over lesser uses for the offending garments. "Use them to mop or dust or pad! Have you not heard of Goonj?" But of course, you will purse your lips in resolute humour and slink away for the sake of peace. What would they know of all that the garment has seen you through? It has the smell and texture of your living, dying moments. It has imprints of all you have loved and lived for. Most of all, more than anything, the garb is easy on you like no one else is. Not even you!

100

The Getaway

Have you ever grinned like a hyena at a traffic policeman who has his pen poised on the challan book? You know you are cooked. Rage sizzles around your edges, but you dare not risk his ego. You are not quite sure what your violation has been, but this man with a hip stuck out has your full attention for now. You are really feeling like a fly. Trapped. There is a meeting you were heading for followed by a dance contest you were to chauffeur your kid to. You have never felt so out of place. A civilized, model citizen with a great faith in the rule of law, you stand there pinching yourself. How could you have brought this moment to pass? You switch your ingratiating grin for a beseeching grimace next. "Madam, you crossed the yellow dividing line to overtake," the pronouncement is made. You kick yourself hard mentally, the mind frantically trying to anticipate the penalty amount even as you wonder sickeningly if there is enough cash in your bag. Quite out of the blue, your rich, Bollywood movies experience comes stealing up to your rescue. You ladle all the helplessness you can muster on to your contrite face and prepare for the impending indignity. "Saab, let me go this time. My first time. I am getting late." Another loose-limbed policeman saunters up. "Your pollution and insurance papers please!" Your back is close to breaking with the mortification now. The thought of the faintly predatory men, flipping through your documents with that brand of smirking suspicion…you just crumble! Without you knowing, your foot creeps up on the throttle, and your limbs ease the car into motion, making an unexpected getaway. You guide the vehicle home with a burning face and a cold body. You were idiot enough to leave your driving licence behind! It was a laminated copy, and they were defaulting you for not carrying the original one. Feeling stupid and close to tears, you slip into your front door, all grim and stony. Alas, the ordeal is not over yet. While the tea brews, you scrounge up your leftover talent to answer the question from the lord and the master, "How did you manage this?"

101

The Game

Have you noticed the tagline? Sports for all, all for sports. Decathlon has transformed staid Indians into preening athletes. We used to play badminton in our front lawns once upon a time in those Bata canvas shoes that came only in two shades, white or khaki. Basketball and throw ball were the other two exciting alternatives. Colony cricket and seven stones and "stappu" were popular too! Everything was clunky and drab. The black Hero cycle, the sombre, brick-coloured basketball, the dull bats, and the far from pink, prim red cricket balls. Skipping ropes were fashioned out of spun chord with colourful wooden grips. And the "lattoo" (spinning top) with that horrendous metal poke had to be coaxed into spinning by a humble cotton string. You would remember the candy-striped, wooden "Pick me up five stones." Chinese Checkers was the fanciest one could get. The dolls all had blue eyes and golden ringlets and dimples in their knees. The Indian versions were fashioned in clay and had spring necks to enthral. There was the inimitable and prosperous "Seth Sethani" couple, bejewelled and robed and nodding away all the way home from the shop you bought them at. You played "Ghar ghar" under makeshift shelters of plywood or old sheets with the all-too-common toy steel utensils. You looked for validation only from your immediate family that loved you and was heavily invested in you. Many naive young people today crave it from the whole world that include dangerous suicide game creators, looking to cleanse society of its worthless members! You moved all your limbs in open spaces, and the sweat rinsed out life's normal choke points. Kids today mostly exercise their fingers, cooped up in their dark rooms, signalling to remorseless raptors with their naive, depressive posts on social media carrying tell-tale hashtags. It used to be about personal hygiene after a hard game. How did you jump to gadget hygiene from there? It used to be just a game. When did it begin to claim promising, young lives?

102

The Distance

Have you ever had your heart run over, watching your child's back move farther and farther away into the distance? You want to snatch her back and never let her go, but her walk is jaunty and purposeful. You know you are doing the right thing, leaving her behind in a fertile soil of ideas and inspiration and resources. You watch her disappear from your sight into a campus where she barely knows a soul, and you cannot bring yourself to move. The cab you ordered draws up, and you stare at the driver's quizzical look. After one last craning of the neck to make sure she is truly gone, you slide into the car with an unfamiliar heaviness. There is a dull, aching edge to the drive back to the hotel, the checking-out formalities, and finally, the boarding for the long flight home. It would have been nice to have had someone pat your back reassuringly or simply shoulder hug you, but the family is wondering what the weight of sorrow is all about, considering how the choice of school has fallen into place. In that acute sense of loss of the parental identity you have lived for seventeen hectic years, you are alone. A fundamental fracture of the self is afoot, and you are hard put to explain. While the pre-flight business runs its course, you wake up to a slow panic rising in your tightening chest. You know you have to take charge before your body hauls itself out of the strapped chair to begin clawing at the locked airplane door. You fix your blind glare at the gleaming tarmac outside your window; there is a drizzle. It is not just your eyes! Frantic with grief, you thrust your hand into your bag to pull out some writing material. You scribble with force, painting a collage of random parenthood flashes with words. By and by, the stabbing soreness abates, and you wonder aloud, "When does the term get over?"

103

The Garbage

Have you ever gotten stuck behind an open garbage truck in bumper-to-bumper traffic? Lethal bits of filth quiver in the wind threateningly. The hapless ones on two wheelers look on in horror, muscles tense should they need to duck dirt and debris. Quite oblivious to the gagging humans shrinking around him, the man steering this obnoxious carriage goes bumping over speed breakers with heart. He is king; there is nothing to lose. But your smug chagrin inside the AC car begins to shatter as a skunky fume steals past tight fittings to assail your upturned nostrils. You shake your head to escape the malodour, but it bravely balloons around you. The car interiors quickly get coated with gunk, forcing you to lower your window just a sliver. You gasp on an acrid nausea brought on by the reeking air. The sourness in that stretch of the road deepens as the red light turns green. There is no way to overtake the bacterial bandwagon. You are stuck behind. The muck ahead begins to bounce again and perilously so. A plastic, sails off the top like a parachute. Peels and rags unfurl untidily. A carton or two go shooting onto the road. Then horror of horrors, a human hand arcs through the air to plunk onto your car bonnet. Rubber burns, metal screeches and doors bang. Imagine the skulduggery. Apparently, the Canter is carrying waste from a city hospital that has won its license without having built an incinerator. Although the garbage is disposed systematically within the hospital in four different coloured bins, the concerned contractor has outsourced its terminal disposal to small time and untrained labour. They merrily overturn the segregated waste onto the same large pile. No processing, only dumping.

104

The Feet

Have you ever struggled with damp toes after a shower, and time and again? You step out into the dressing room, feeling newly minted, all primed for the body lotion and the hair drier. A quick glance at the clock and you hurry through, nice and smooth, with the draping and the painting routine. But the feet! They are never dry enough at that penultimate stage for the ceremonial footwear. It is too wet inside the bath to wipe them dry thoroughly. By the time you make it to the dressing room, you have already consigned the main towel to the laundry. You are also, no longer athletic enough to lift your toes to a tiny hand towel. After some lurching and stumbling and grabbing at curtains for support, good lord, you look around for a potential fabric surface. The bed is beyond the latched door, you could have guiltily dragged your soles on the counter pane. The shoes are new, and you hate treating them to unnecessary moisture. You flex your extremities and trail them up and down your calves, trying to get some dampness off. *Dry enough*, you tell yourself before thrusting them into the footwear. There will be time in the car to fan out the toes for an airing. You laugh silently as the vehicle slides past Independence Day floral roundels and tricolour panels on way to the Red Fort. Russell B. Long's quote has come to mind: "Democracy is like a raft; it won't sink, but you will always have your feet wet."

105

The Celebrity

Have you ever shrunk from a celebrity? Hung back awkwardly? Most others around you are taking up strategic points so as to catch the maximum rays off the rising sun. Some good friends even beckon you close, but you go shuffling three feet forward and four back. You feel a sheepish annoyance at yourself. What, after all, are you? A reverse snob? "No, no, I would rather be great myself than chase autographs of the celebrated. I mean, I have it all. It is just the stars in my chart that are holding me back, an astrological matter of degrees." Is that what you are telling yourself? Or are you wondering what is to be gained from two seconds of face to face, if that happens at all, with the country's who's who? Does their gold or good luck rub off on you in that faintest of proximity? Of course, you admire their accomplishments and marvel at their destiny. You applaud their creativity and take your hat off to their discipline. But glory by proxy? Via a selfie or a handshake or even folding hands. All those faces you see on TV and magazines and in the movies, they are regular humans with the same business of living to get on with as the rest of us. If anything, their lives appear tougher; the stakes are higher. They are probably hard put to keep it together and remain whole through the fame and success. Why, then, would you want a piece of them?

The Lighting

Have you used dim lighting to showcase your drawing room as richer and more tastefully done than it actually is? A name that it gets from the "withdrawing room" of the 16th century, the drawing room is probably the smartest and the most useless of your rooms. It is your badge, your signature, your telling front. It is also the room that you least live in. The prettiest and most expensive home trappings you own are for the visiting guests. You have poured quite a bit of yourself into the curtain fabric, the sofa set, the large Buddha mural, and all the marble consoles. The glass case displaying delicate curios and your prized crystal sourced from distant lands reflect your travel trails. Carefully placed lamps and tea light shades cast their soft glow to give the room its classic vintage look. Flourishing little plants in smart earthenware pretty much conclude the classy cosiness. Ironically, however, your cultured home style holds good only under a subdued lighting. Unknown to your guests, the green onyx candle tree has been fixed together with Fevi Kwik. The silk carpet is patched up down below with cleverly tacked strips of buckram fabric. An expensive Turkish plate is placed just so; a chip has come off one edge. It happens. There is the inevitable damage in the umpteen number of postings and moves you labour through. So, what do you do? You get creative as best you can and pray that the man of the house will refrain from playing piano on the switchboards just as the guests are making to seat themselves. Guess what? He does not disappoint. You grit your teeth and seethe as the lights come on one after another to wreck the delusion you had so carefully cultivated. Dim them, please, the lights!

The Deliverance

Have you heaved a massive sigh of relief at the rain that came down just as you were making way to step out for a walk? It absolved you of the guilt had you just listened to your heart that was crying to stay home and be lazy. Such a relief, these unexpected deliverances. Remember that time you had promised to show up for a friend's workshop? Imagine your delirium when the political opposition party declared a "Delhi bandh" on that very hour and day. Such a sneaky relief! Your enthusiasm is usually inversely proportional to the event schedule. The closer you get to the date, the faster your bluff and bluster fade. About a safe month away, your magnanimity literally brims over. "Of course, I will be joining in. Are you kidding me? No question!" As the event draws close, you find yourself rapidly losing interest. The day before, you begin inventing excuses. And then something happens to save you and leave you guilt free! Life is full of such saving graces. You haven't done your homework one day, and your class teacher happens to take the day off. You are going cross-eyed over a Wednesday deadline, and you suddenly learn the function has been called off. You have planned to sit up, cooking late night, and the expected house guest informs of a last-minute change of plans. You are not mean enough to rejoice in convenient coincidences! But you do appreciate inertia and begin to understand the futility of stressing and palpitating over non-issues. The best laid plans of mice and men often go awry. Let's just not stop until we are proud.

The Band

Have you ever had to mount a near perfect event by proxy on a 'value for money' budget? You have no real authority to start with. Your relevance is dependent on something as ephemeral as courtesy. You function on the clay feet of legacy, mainly a polite institutional permission to play a role. Needless to say, you will need the alertness and peripheral smarts of a tightrope walker who spins a pompom on the head for added effect. A band of women such as this exists. They smile a lot. It masks the occasional flicker of steel. They come hard wired to put on a show. It is something they have grown up watching their predecessors do. Their experience gives them enough frames of references to spot the red flags. They place the bar high. Their expectations come couched in words of suggestions and recommendations. All this happens behind a deceptively calm exterior. As few words as possible, an expectant body language, and a disarming countenance. Their obsessive preoccupation with detail perhaps springs from the deep-seated insecurity of knowing how fragile and second-hand their control is. It could give way any moment under the pressure of human emotions. Personal admiration, thoughtful disposition, and a mature ability to ignore a whole lot does eventually get them ready cooperation. Despite some views and perceptions to the contrary, there is a huge amount of institutional pride involved. A sense of belonging. An identity born of close community living. Come what may, they will do what they do with panache. Is it any wonder then that they applaud so enthusiastically and express gratitude so profusely? They know what it takes. Could you, dear lady, reading this, be of and from this band?

109

The Ambivalent

Have you ever had FB dismissed within your hearing in a faintly self-righteous tone? "I am not on Facebook and all; I keep away from this type of stuff, baba!" Your toes curl at the implied disapproval. The ears almost singe. You beat back the oncoming wave of tentative shame. Your weak smile belies the fact that you indeed are all over the Facebook. A perfectly ripe case for psychoanalysis! You simply have to announce your movements every single day to the whole world even if they are just crawls from one movie hall to another gallery. Your friends know exactly how long you have been off your bicycle. They can tell you have been shamming on your golf too. You get your share of private messages. "Hey, is all well with you?" So, what's so improper thus far? Then you have heard it said in your vicinity: "I read and watch all that the others post, but I don't comment and all." Like wearing dark glasses, one stares but one doesn't get caught. Sweet! But *you* know you have been guilty of being out there. Of engaging, refuting, appreciating, annoying, debating. You have to acknowledge it is an ambivalent medium. There are things you post you would not dream of saying face to face. You give yourself away in unforeseen ways. At times, some posts reflect major upheavals afoot without the person posting, intending it. The FB finally functions in different ways for different age groups. In your fifties, is it a shout of desperation? As if to say, "I have still got some juice left; watch me reclaim my potential that I presumably put on hold." Or is it a bid for returning love and attention to yourself, independent of the roles you played in life? What, in any case, is so repugnant about connecting with long lost friends, playing peek-a-boo with family and dishing out some food for thought? Delicious, devilish, drama is your FB. Almost human.

The Resolve

Have you taken important people in your life for granted until they seemed caught in peril and then you woke up all of a sudden? An image of life without them clutched at your heart like a vice. "Oh my God, what am I going to do without them?" An onslaught of guilt. A caveat of fear. A rush of self-preservation. The rabbit hole of regret. No, you have not ill-treated them, not at all. You have just been living your life by a "to-do" list that did not even feature them. "They can wait" has been the sentiment around your shared spaces with them. There will be enough time, you think. Someday, when you have earned certainty and closure around the rest of the compulsory chaos, you will come clean with your primary support system. Those human beings, who have given you the gift of trust and dependability that leaves you enough energy for negotiating your daily events, are not going anywhere you think. Their discipline, their consistency, their integrity is not running out on you any time soon. They stand by, never demanding so much as an atom of you. And secure in their presence, you explore yourself, pushing your envelope, experimenting with authentic living, little knowing how few receive that luxury in life. Then one day, in the hospital, sitting outside the operation theatre, you feel like you have been hit by a demonetized truck. That pillar in your life is lying horizontal inside. The familiar booming voice is fighting anaesthesia. You feel dark and unclean, dredging up flashes of neglect you have reserved for them in the past. You make yourself promises. Never again. Enough of these lessons. You will make sure your loved ones know they are loved. You will value all you have. Weeks drag by. The personal peril eventually sets. And you are back soon enough to being yourself. Or are you?

111

The Smile

Have you any idea how different you look outside the home? Your genuine glum, home face is replaced with a radiating smile that nearly makes it to the eyes. Your social armour of happy courtesy and careful words is in place. You throw back your head and laugh even. The greetings burst with cheer as do your cheek muscles. You want it known, clear as crystal, that you are doing splendidly. You were taught that celebration brought friends while desolation was lived alone. You saw your parents put on a brave face and soldier through life's drama with grit and grace. It was bad form, moreover, to unburden on mere acquaintances and social friends. With them, you made small talk and appeasing sounds. The limited emotional fare that survived structured family norms was reserved for the four walls. There was a clear-cut boundary delineating home from the world outside. Perhaps there was a silent disengagement amongst specific members in a family. Some would have quit mentally but stayed! In fact, there was barely any great premium on smiling back then. Remember the black and white portraits of our mothers and aunts and grandmothers. Do you recall seeing their pearlies flash? A feminine smile was viewed with suspicion once. Mona Lisa's smile continues to be under debate and discussion. You have come a long way since to the barrage of positive urgings today to smile often and wider. Use your smile to change the world, you are told. "Smile while you still have teeth" is an oft repeated suggestion. Peace begins with a smile, didn't you know?! A smile is the prettiest thing you can wear, particularly if you are a woman; sexism be damned. It is as though no one has heard of the phenomenon of smiling depression! At times, blessings may feel like a burden to some. *Tum itna jo muskura rahe ho…*

112

The Homecoming

Neither blood nor business and certainly not, just good old bonhomie. A place! A mere place can sometimes hold people together if they spent their childhood there, amidst a forest as zealous as their parents. Pachmarhi is the name. Fairy pool. Haandi Kho. Pandav Caves. Shaily Mathur. Amarjeet Singh Malik. And the Army Education Corp. None of the braggadocio of hardcore combatant paltans but a community bond to rival the best of them. That is the AEC centre and its corollary, the Kendriya Vidyalaya, Pachmarhi (KVP). Was it the physical isolation of this plateau of humanity? Could it have been the social somnolence brought on by the vaporous fragrance of the mahua flower? Perhaps, it was the intimate size of the cantonment or the charming ghats on the drive up from Pipariya. Maybe the lyrical names of the centre's constituent companies such as Tithwal or Chushul or Burki. Or the intrepid band of parents with their *fauji* culture of esprit de corps evident in the qawaalis, the skits, the tambola nights, and that *holi* madness they co-created with an unfailing regularity. Memories remained constant and consistent. Birthday parties, picnics, nature trails, hockey matches, western music appreciation evenings, NCC jamboree, fancy dress competitions, cycle rides, skating sessions, air gun *shikaars*, ghost story hideouts, and dancing in the club. One couldn't have asked for a shinier childhood. So, there we were at a recent reunion, gazing at one another with those tireless smiles, the spouses looking on askance. What sentiment could possibly string together several generations across the normal business of living? Pachmarhi aka Enid Blyton's Peterswood. And our beloved veterans, who got their shots of life, just watching their next three generations chirp, in so trusting a space of connectedness. Life sings a pure song every once in a while.

113

The Flight

Sunshine can take many shapes. It could be a thoughtful hand on the elbow while negotiating a dug-up road. A microwaved Choco Pie with its turgid heart of cream. Also, a regression to childish lisping with the parents occasionally. And who is not warmed by a trusting assent coming from the progeny to family plans? There may be a polite resistance to micro-managing from the hovering parents, yes, but there is also an open sharing of fears and insecurities. The sun truly shines on way home from a shopping trip, eyes lit up with the pleasure of prosperity and affordability. A word of gratitude from one's child is that silken bow on the box of parenting joy. Sunshine is in sharing a Mysore *masala dosa* across a light-dappled window table at the Ashok Samrat Hotel, discussing life plans and *gyan*. There is strawberry crush ice cream in the freezer, the cheerful radiator plugged into position, fresh baking afoot. And then all too quickly, it is time for her fifteen hours long return flight. Your heart quakes at the distance involved. You put life on hold until the flight tracker confirms her plane landed forty-five minutes early. You then shut your eyes quickly and open them, scared at the panic that might set in over just how far she has gone. With time, the keen sense of her absence will dullen. You will gather the courage to Skype with her without wanting to break through the laptop glass so as to snatch her back. She has flown. Your nest is empty again. You, it is you who gave her wings.

114

The Outrage

We are like that only! All kinds of emotional drama are acceptable barring one. I have not seen outrage at shabby output. Poor quality performance is rued only in our sportspersons. But a sub-standard professional product is tolerated, even expected of most of the rest of us. Slouching, lethargic guards at our gates. Forgetful and unhygienic waiters. Casual, reckless cab drivers. Lackadaisical salesmen. Gossipy, distracted gym trainers. Tip hungry but casual salon stylist. We abound in these "absent in their presence" professionals. Like a disease, our unprofessional work output sucks the life out of our environment, but it remains mysteriously unchallenged. So endemic is the below par performance that the rare brilliance hurts, nay threatens. If you are punctual and keep your word and, God forbid, write notes of appreciation, someone soon enough will demand to know, "Have you lived or worked abroad?!" What is our shared history and culture that makes a clinical efficiency so foreign to us? We can grin and bear delays, messy confusion, even a no-show, but a demanding client or a kickass delivery stump us completely. It robs us of our magnanimity towards the tardiness of others. What connection would you possibly have with someone who demands and delivers with aplomb? We have a term for this kind of conduct. It is called "setting a bad example." And God help you if you castigated anyone for their shoddy work. You are gathering bad karma for yourself. Beware the turn of the wheel of fortune.

115

The Investment

It is our highest ever gamble. A child's wedding! In no other life's venture are we as heavily invested. Our reason for existence is on show with this one gala. It displays what we have done with our lives thus far. The social sanction and the approval it is sure to earn us is equivalent to a holy dip. With this one family event, we hope to absolve ourselves, to make it to the conclusive league, to arrive. But weddings, like life, bring surprises. The biggest culprits are the family members themselves, the second- and third-tier lot. Thanks to them, the marriage ends up not being so much about the couple as about these fretful folks. They seem to come with their little black books, noting down the misdemeanours, the lapses, the oversights, the loops, and the holes. The show is the clan nit-picker's haven. And the nose-saver's arena. Then there are the guests, lined up at the dais, shifting aching feet in impossible heels. They smile on autopilot at the multiple cameras and stumble back into the comfort of the food stalls. The salad table at a wedding feast is one place where the fresh looks stale. Everything is rich and laden with sin. The tamarind chutney is too synthetic, hot-off-the-oven breads being the saving grace. The servers sleepwalk. You can't put it past them to pluck a cherry off the dessert cake with their backs turned. There is a pervasive air of bounty fatigue. People don't know one another. Most overeat and scramble home in relief from the bling and ruckus. It is the marriage season! And purse strings are opening. May all flourish! And while you are there, take care with those masticated missiles from jabbering mouths leaning in to be heard over the aggressive music.

116

The Maxim

The bars have shifted more in this one generation than with any other preceding swathe of worthies. From bringing fame to the family, it has become about personal fulfilment. It used to be about being an asset to the community. We are happy today if our young are able to acquire a semblance of self-sufficiency. Times were when men and women grappled with death and disease and deprivation to create wealth. You are lucky today if your offspring does not take you to the laundromat, for dressing them up as a sweeper in their school fancy dress. Private spaces behind tightly shut doors did not exist in Indian homes until some years ago. Personal preferences at regular meals were unheard of. The menu would be decided by the mother in the kitchen, and everyone ate the same food. Family adults made gifts of clothes that were gamely put to use by the juniors. Clans entertained themselves as a unit. It never occurred to any of us that we could be out doing our own thing instead of listening to the repetitive stories of our patriarch. Parents knew best. Grandparents had to be served. And aunts and uncles had both a stake and a say. Then along came the gales of change. Individuality, personal space, liberty of choice, unconstitutional fraternity of peers, impatience with cultural inertia…we began to buffet in the crashing all around us, grabbing at straws, fighting to keep our heads above water. Rue the global influences next? Blame ourselves for diluting our authority and not using our influence effectively enough? Or wake up and smell the threatening coffee of break-neck change. For all the flak Indian parents get for being repressive and controlling and ambitious… there aren't many with as serious a parenting culture as ours. Meanwhile, has anyone worked out how much co-signing is involved in that modern maxim called unconditional love?

The Square

Can you say 'sex' without dipping your voice or casting a quick look around? Have you ever lost control of your senses and passed out over the table, on the floor, in a car? You couldn't possibly have been out ever on the city roads, alone at half past one in the morning. Surely you know how to spell the word "pleasure"! And what were you doing in your teens if not experimenting? You ever challenged the norm? Taken a risk? Followed your heart? Worn it on the sleeve? Had your heart broken? Walked in the Pride Parade. Smoked a joint. Stayed up the entire night watching Netflix? Been high on endless cups of coffee? Mouthed a word stronger than "shoot"? Explored an alternate lifestyle? Spouted existential angst? What a wastrel, you! What good are you then, as a modern parent? A useless goody shoe. No frame of reference, you good for nothing adult. Good luck, therefore, with your empty, airy advisories in that long winded vocabulary of yours. That *gyan* does not apply. It is irrelevant. Everybody agrees that our young know best! And even if you thought otherwise, well, who wants to open their mouth and then be blamed for the rest of their miserable years. A potential alienation, the effort involved in keeping pace with our young, the risk of being unpopular with them, a desire to be perceived as their friend far more than a mere parent…we drown our nagging concerns in the universal cacophony over the superior smarts of the young. Well, wisdom is something else! And that comes only with age. So go on, hang in there, be the square you are, nice and stubborn.

118

The Balcony

Have you ever peered at a theatre production through a pair of balcony railings? It costs only 500 rupees. If you are lucky, the middle rod would be broken to give you an unrestricted view of the stage. The experience is heightened and particularly sensory should you go by yourself. The ticket person turns your solo booking around, confirming in that bemused tone that you are indeed alone on the trip. You are tempted to share all the thinking that went into clicking on the unit sandwich seat featured on BookMyShow. You couldn't bring yourself to disrupt the odd double seats marked green on the seating plan. *Why spoil someone's fun?* you had told yourself. And it is good to attend events alone occasionally. The solitary anonymity is restful. You can curl back into your chair and literally disappear in the darkened hall. You can regress. You can dissolve. You can cry. You can tap your feet. You can nod your head. There is no pressure to be visible. You are unseen. The hush inside is oddly respectful. The murmur strangely considerate. The sharing is instant. There, on the stage, is a purer, perfect extraction of what it is to be a human being. Every sound touches you richer and fuller. The lights create illusions that are starker than all that is ordinary about me and you. The air has a dab of coffee, some flecks of popcorn. The carpets gulp down footfalls. In rare moments, the audience pulls their hands out to clap with conviction. When the curtain comes down, your escape is up. You come home, reminding yourself that in life, you don't wait for the storm to pass. You just go out into the rain and dance.

The Star

Have you felt an inexplicable sense of loss at the passing away of a film star who defined your adolescent years? It does not matter that you did not know the actor personally. You knew the magic he created with his movies. Shashi Kapoor had that smile, with just the barest narrowing of his eyes under that lifted brow. Not to forget the cocking of his head. And that little skippity hop with hands tied behind his back. Jennifer Kendal, Nafisa Ali, Kunal Kapoor, 36 Chowringhee Lane, and Vijeta made his story bigger and brighter. In *Kabhi Kabhie*, he had me on his team rather than the dark and dour Bachchan. And I wondered always at the spunk and sparkle of the Kapoor clan. What karmic calculation concentrated so much talent and looks in one DNA? And why did their success not guard them against latter day obesity, for one. What a gentleman though, this Shashi Kapoor, smashingly likeable. The skating sequence in *Aa Gale Lag Jaa* with Sharmila Tagore and the hide and seek with Rakhee in *Sharmeelee* are some delightful bits of the Shashi Kapoor collage that brought me cosy thrills. They enchant us with their portrayals on screen, our Bollywood stars, replete with their signature style and presence. I would be lesser for not having seen the easy charm and graceful empathy of Shashi Kapoor on screen. He clearly worked hard. He had the conviction to cross over in cinema. He had the talent to shine in a brilliant family. What happened to his health, one wonders! Rest in peace, Capt. Ajit Kapoor.

120

The Offering

Have you ever winced at being offered prasad? You will, of course, not refuse. Even as your mind brakes mid-flow with a no, you stick your palms out automatically, right one up. The head, ever so dips. We have an inbuilt switch that summons the look of reverence in seconds. Our waists fold on autopilot! There is a strangely still connection between you and the giver. Without examining it closely, you pop the invariably damp object into your mouth. There is mutual relief at the ritual done. With this one exchange, we give our ancient culture a puff of breath. Come to think of it, what a magnanimous and benevolent practice. It is a spiritual amplification of our prayer having been accepted for consideration by our deity. And by distributing the blessed offering, we create a domino manifestation for ourselves. Every recipient of our prasad adds their might to our prayer. In this exchange of potency, there is hope and an optimistic faith. *Ladoo, appam, panchamirtham, batasha, powa, modaka,* tulsi leaves, *boondhi, sweet pongal, kadha parshad,* noodles, alcohol…flowers, *vibhuti, sindoor,* talismans, chunnis, sarees, *rudraksha…*the range is simply stunning. The Food Safety and Standards Authority of India (FSSAI), however, wants the edible offerings to come under the government scanner so as to ensure hygiene and health of the consumers. Interestingly, there is a push in some parts of our country, like Uttaranchal, to have women make healthier and more eco-friendly prasad, using organic produce from local farmers such as *chaulai,* baby corn, dry fruits, and ghee. Meanwhile, there are the sealed packets of prasad brought back by friends and family from their spiritual sojourns. What, pray, might be the protocol for leftover prasad?

V

EVEN ODDS

The DNA

Have you had a candid friend tell you, "Oh my God, you look so much better now! I remember thinking what has she done to herself! Your half grey mop nearly gave me a heart attack"? We as a people can be quite intrusive, particularly with those we consider close. Prematurely grey hair, thickness of your ankles, the knotty fingers, bulbous nose, ample bottoms are all grist for the family and friendly mill. It is perfectly normal for both the paternal and maternal roots to lay claim on broad foreheads, almond-shaped eyes, clear skin, and lustrous hair. Allergies, bunions, wobbly dentals, knocking knees…heaven forbid, let these go abegging. Not our superior genes! It must be them! Was it sweet mother nature's self-preservation trick to have us all bask in the glow of our robust genetic stock? And how is it that most families lay claim to a stunningly beautiful ancestor and a highly principled forefather against the backdrop of prosperous resources that were lost in some unfortunate incident or the other. Ancestors are larger than life in our clan consciousness. Good for us. Their genes give us a sense of continuity and belonging. It is an oddly comforting feeling to gaze at your grandparents' portraits and see yourself reflected in their faces. DNA has a very sharp memory. It may skip generations at times; it may create interesting combinations so that a daughter takes after the father and the son resembles his mother; some features may stubbornly spring up generation after another. Family lore abounds in the hits and the misses. So how have you done in the genetic lottery?

122

The Learner

Have you noticed the cap we put on learning with life's milestones? Marriage for women and professional self-sufficiency for men have traditionally meant brakes on pro-active learning. Of course, you learn along the way, you absorb from around you, you go through the mandated motions, but you stop the active, energetic, self-driven seeking of your student life before. Age is supposed to let us off the mental, physical, and emotional rigor involved in learning a new skill. In time, you come to have professional success and well brought-up kids and a beautiful house and decent investments and an extended family, cooing grudging approval. Now, why in the world then would you still not sit back and relax? What is all this enrolling in courses and classes you don't stand a chance of putting to use, considering as you are, past your mid-life? It must be some sort of low self-esteem; your folks may likely wonder. Could you be trying to escape from a very basic sadness in all the flitting from one classroom to another? Perhaps, you are still seeking some form of approval from those close to you. That is how pathetic you are! No contentment, just whirring around like a headless chicken. Learning is, moreover, not generally viewed in the same league as more acceptable hobbies like reading and music. It is not vague enough. It calls for commitment and investment and consistency. It is more important today than ever before. Today, you need to remain an asset all your life. Learning is no longer for life. Learning is life.

123

The Wish

Have you ever sat down and given a thought to whether you will leave behind a chaos or a sense of order and ease? As the chins multiply in number and the bones go porous, you wonder at the time left. Science has declared that humans have hit the ceiling as far as life span and qualities of the heart and mind go. This is as far as we go in biological development. Given that you are nifty long enough to negotiate the smog, hijacks, cancers, traffic accidents, political skulduggery, betrayals, terrorist attacks, and Arnab Goswami…the life expectancy is still finite. And like it or not, you will be leaving behind those *kundan* danglers of yours, those diaries you have been filling up, that apartment you slaved after, the mutual investments, and the odd bitcoin fantasy. You could also potentially leave behind hurt lifetimes and bitter beings and fraternal feuds with your emotional decisions on nominees and the like. Oh no! Not one of us believes we may not have time enough to clear up after us. But experience says otherwise. It seems smart, more and more, to speak up when you are cogent and your environment receptive. Family is about festivities and retirement planning, yes, but it is also about the protection of their dignity and the upholding of yours when the time comes. Do you want to spend your final days at the mercy of hospital staff, a poked and pinched carcass, your loved ones heartbreakingly out of your reach? Do you want the family to celebrate your years with them rather than bemoan your loss months on end after you have beaten your retreat? To make your wishes known and to organize your affairs in a fair and loving manner would qualify as the toughest but the greatest gift we can leave each other.

124

The Battle

Have you marvelled at how primed we are for battle through the day? Our eyes and ears are peeled for disaster in waiting, our muscles coiled for conflict. You are prepared for the worst. A hotel booking might be missing your name, the flight coordinator may have mistaken an "S" for a "5" in your PNR number. You may be kept standby on the cruise passenger list despite a confirmation having been sent earlier. In this part of the world, you set out every day, negotiating skirmishes. The women ingratiate themselves with service providers to eke out what ought to have been a given. The men lose their cool or place calls to their human networks. We are used to hard-won combats in daily life. What would the jaded folks living their way of life in the developed world and brought up on the numbing effect of social security know about the thrill of cutting lines, negotiating a fifty-rupee rebate, beating someone else to the cab, bullying your way to better seats, wangling a dolphin sighting, or leveraging on a ride with a wrested freebie such as a tour of the pilot cabin! We are the natives of a former colony. Nothing may be presumed as a given. We are grateful if the meal we paid for with the GST tax turns out to our satisfaction. We are thrilled if our uteruses survive the bad roads we paid for in taxes. We don't complain about having to beach it out amidst filthy flotsam and touristy debris. We don't lodge complaints over unserviceable TVs and intercoms in suites sold to us as "Royal Palaces". We, in fact, empathize with the owner. He is just eight months short of his lease expiry, poor fellow. He will obviously ease off on the services! It is enough that the staff does not say no and keeps insisting all is well. That is all we ask for. Assurances! So fortunate that no one paints us the true picture. We wouldn't survive it.

The Wipe

Have you ever been asked why Indian women have the world's most gorgeous hair? While the globe marvels at the magic of coconut oil and *shikakai* rinses, little would they know the uses we put our tresses to! Many a full maternal heart has swiped kohl off the eye, dabbed it onto her "*Gunchi Papchi*" and wiped the fingertip clean on her own crown. The kohl is not counted as an objectionable blob. It is close to our hearts, so much a part of our culture. Kohl signifies our shy, almond-shaped dark eyes; a dab of it is our talisman against misfortunes. Kajal is full-bodied like an eye pencil can never be. And it goes on our hair! Ditto for ink stains from the nearly defunct fountain pens and the modern gel contraptions. Which true blue desi has not wiped indigo stains off his writing fingers onto his scalp? Ink is a venerated fluid. It is the makings of knowledge, a tool of Goddess Saraswati, and it integrates beautifully with our locks. Paan! That delicious, punchy, sweet leaf pouch of rich spices and seeds and juices. After you have safely tucked it into the pocket of your cheek, where do you wipe clean the minty cool coating left behind on your fingertips? A few quick stabs at the hair, but naturally. Oh, we do fine, not wasting rolls and rolls of tissue paper too, thus saving valuable tree barks. The heads that dip at the Gurudwara also carry the gleam off the ghee in the prasad. Having popped the last bolus of that delicious halwa into the mouth, watch the devotees rub their greasy hands over the hair on their forearms, finishing with a final flourish over their beards. Love is truly in our hair!

126

The Gaze

Have you ever felt eyes boring into you? Your back, your shoulders, your silhouette. Not lecherous or with any other mal-intent. But just watching. Observing. Noting. Even wondering maybe. You swivel your head to pin the owners of those piercing saucers, but no one is looking. They all seem absorbed in their own affairs. You turn back sheepishly to the task at hand, but your skin begins to pimple up again. You straighten up and wonder. You have clearly not bargained for all the shiny surfaces in your shared spaces. There are burnished doors, glass partitions, metallic covers, furniture beadings, chrome curios, polished clay creations. These grab what is around them and hold it for the observant gazes. Those reflective things give it all away; they are the stealth periscopes of people-watchers. Consider the possibilities! You can keep an eye on the kitchen happenings from your safe perch in the dining hall. It is possible to minimize social-networking windows before the boss walks in your door and is upon you. Imagine the gardener's surprise at being called out on his squirreling even though you had your back towards him. It is no secret humans have been watching humans forever. The practice just fell out of favour under the newly fangled notions of privacy and personal space. But the good news is that people-watching is rapidly losing its creepy scent. It is the stated hobby of many all over the world today. Find a nice location, sit back, and be natural in your scanning. You will learn about people, their culture, and their environment. There is no escaping. And we have a word for the really close-range watching we do online. Stalking!

127

The Listener

Have you lately photo-finished your say because you can see your listener no longer able to hold his? He cannot wait to shoot at the mouth. In fact, he hasn't heard a word you spoke from the heart. He was half-listening to you. There was so much he was dying to tell you about that time he experienced the exact same thing as you. There were umpteen solutions he had to offer you. He knew of several people who had been to the same place as you. He got you. He heard you. If only you would shut up and let him speak now. God, are you ever going to give him the space for interjection? In 2018, the stress is in getting a word in from down under, forget sideways. No one even pretends to be contrite about interrupting. Times were when polite folks murmured in a subdued tone, "I am sorry to interrupt but…" We are cutting animated speakers off today and appropriating their targets unabashedly for reception of our own monologues. We are convinced no one can tell us a new story. We have been there. We have done that. Don't we know it all? And our own shoes are so much cosier. No way are we putting ourselves into another's. So here we are, a bunch of vain, self-centred, futile blatherers, petrified of losing control. Or of not being able to complete our delivery. Or of diluting our identity. Or not achieving our objectives. Of course, talking seems of greater value than listening. Talking at about two-hundred plus words per minute, we are not listening to ourselves either. We are busy wasting the unimaginable power of our silence. If only we would get busier listening, we would hear not only what is being said but also what is not! There is only one way to cut through the noise and get to the truth. Be quiet first!

The Signature

Have you stepped back and taken a long hard look at yourself on occasions? Oh no, it is not all your fault. You are a product of centuries of racial genetic transfer. But, of course, you have no idea where you have got those peculiar quirks and mannerisms from. You don't remember anyone sitting you down for a lesson. And yet, here you are, one of a kind. No one in the world can stick that bindi as strategically as you do on to the beadings of various mirrors. Your trick of spit-wetting paper money and book leaves deserves patenting. Ah, for that tell-tale swipe on the fabric over your bottom after a wash job. You are the absolute bane of hand towels. You stun with your talent for utilizing your space and what's on your person. You have swiped a child's face with the corner of your *dupatta*. You have equalized tea you just poured into cups with a tea spoon. Next, you have proceeded to run your fingers over a washed steel spoon before offering it to a guest. You are cute! You run around thrusting extra body lotion squirts on your palm at your progeny. For all your talk of public hygiene, it is perfectly forgivable to make a kid squat anywhere green and leafy for a quick relief job. And those stuffed suitcases you sit on to close…shut them with your heavier kin lending weight. You know all the theory on the green earth but catch you throwing away a single carry bag. You tuck them away unfailingly for future use. You also store magazines with intentions of making paper beads with the brilliantly coloured glossy paper. When out with family, a male member will squeeze past and over to seat himself next to another male occupying a seat. You store used-up cells and batteries with some vague plan of squeezing the last of them in future. Who has not reserved a place with a hanky, a programme card, or a Bisleri! You bow your head to orange stones under trees. It is always the company your child keeps that is suspect. Your darling is a pristine babe. You take a garbage heap as a licence to garnish it with some of your own refuse. In the normal course, you judge others keenly, but there are two occasions you will forgive them anything for: a marriage in the family or a bereavement. While the world researches the great Indian head bobble, let's just focus on demolishing those *pani puris*. Slurp!

129

The Lie

Have you ever used a word other than "fine" to the polite query, "How are you doing?" Imagine the shock on the enquirer's face were you to be honest in your response! "I am miserable; my cat has abandoned me," for one. How about "I can't think straight. My husband is diabetic but will not stop eating sweets." Or, "I am sick and tired of my bulging stomach. I hate attending fancy events, looking the way I do." You could well come clean with "I am struggling in my interaction with my adult children." Would the heavens fall with these gritty admissions? Would our listener judge us, think lesser of us, or begin to give advice? One doesn't know because one hasn't tried. It is not considered polite or appropriate to admit that not all is fine. It is viewed as some form of intrusion on the other's time, a cry for help, an admission of weakness, a crack in the barely sane facade. And so everyone goes around assuring everyone else how fantastic life is, and in the bargain, the pain behind the polite cheer continues to simmer and turn toxic. We have cultivated this dishonest idea of infallibility that does not sit well with the human condition. Humans have to constantly fight inertia, self-doubt, anger, ill health, and more. But we have been brought up to soldier on, maintain a stoic front, and be positive. It also keeps us cosy and useless doing nothing spectacular because well, all is fine. It does not help to have the human mind kill all good ideas within seconds of them bubbling up in our heads. We have mastered the art of thinking ourselves out of new things to do and try. Why...all is so fine no, right?

The Expert

Have you ever received dieting advice from an over-weight well-wisher? A cardiologist may have taken a smoking break in your periphery! How about a real estate broker who has never owned a house himself? There are therapists spouting diagnosis from their personally-troubled perches. Even Freud, for all the ammunition he left the psych community with could not "cure" his own daughter of lesbianism! Who hasn't survived religious fanatics at home with hearts as closed as a government office on the weekend? The digital literacy has made this phenomenon happier. Back then, only the Reader's Digest used to be quoted for illustration and by the select few who read it. Today, the experts are crawling out of frames and beadings. We have all "surfed, self-informed, read, and converted" in the soft pool of our bedside lamps, hunched over our TABs and Laptops and Smartphones. The virtual world enjoys a greater credibility with us than our own eyes and gut. How many times have you reached a spot and shaken your head in disbelief because the GPS insists your destination is at least eighty meters away? Traditions seem comic, our immediate family is not with it enough, the experts are obviously not practicing what they preach…we place our faith in online wisdom put there by strangers looking for business. Of course, there is a lot of information and ease of transaction and empowering communication Google favours us with. But the monster is not invested in any of us personally. On crucial life conflicts, it will tell us exactly what we want to hear. You can pretty much rationalize any and every one of your pet notions out there in the online court. You come away feeling in the right. This expert is not your grandma to say to you, "Don't smoke, drink or have free sex!"

131

The Generation

Have you met anyone socially and not asked them what their children do? Our culture tells us that the kids are our most visible validation. Their success and failure are ours. Our primary duty is to facilitate and support them until our last breath. Anything we do for ourselves has to come after their needs have been met. It is fairly common to base retirement plans on the needs of our children. We want to continue to be available to them long past a reasonable expectation and even desire, in some cases. There is an active myopia amongst parents today that will not permit them to see that their progeny may be crying for space and independence and liberty. Freedom to be average. To live life from a backpack. To roam around the world. To not shoulder family baggage. To just be, for heaven's sake! To shake off the suffocating stranglehold of religion. To run from the forced socializing with extended family. To be released of expectations. To not have to plan, project, invest, save. To not be knocked down by a mace called marriage. To not bring kids into this world and give them the uninformed parenting they were themselves subjected to. To earn just enough. To not repay house and car loans. To not lose steam in the rat race. To not have to worry about standing out. To shun brilliance for contentment. To reject competition for an inclusive mediocrity. To listen only to the music of their own hearts. To drop the mask and be themselves. To be able to scream, abuse, love, and experiment. To take risks. What's wrong with that? You grew up in an age of meagre means. They have matured being waited upon by proud parents and grandparents. Don't cry now. You enabled the magnificent millennial and GenZ. iGen and Gen Alpha to follow!

The Fear

Have you any memory of when this insidious emotion seeped into you? This dark, acidic, bile coloured thing called fear. Do you even remember a time when you were young and fearless? Nothing bad could ever happen to you. Then you became a parent! That new little life sucked out all your bravado, turning you into a perpetually on-edge, dithering duh. You have lain awake at night since. You have spent hours staring vacantly at the clock, numb at the disastrous thoughts swimming around your head while the kid is out on the city roads in the middle of the night. You have dialled, then disconnected their number thirty-two times, sick at the switched-off tone. The once potent and flourishing 'you' has acquired an abiding faith in the worst-case scenario. You latch your suitcase with a thick metal chain in the First AC now. You cover your jewellery with a scarf or a dupatta when out. You submit yourself to medical checks regularly. You track your children like a hound. You plan and string up several standby options. You subscribe to insurance plans. You suffer anxiety at the smallest plan going awry. Some fears are specific in these parts. Your cup of tea may run cold. The gulab jamun may not be served hot. Your weekend movie booking may come up against a houseful sign. Your maid may vanish for days without notice. Your child may be unmarried at 30 years. You just might bump into a relative when between jobs. God forbid, should India lose to Pakistan! What are we to do with ourselves? The air rings with well-meaning dictums, "Be careful. Don't get run over, mugged, hijacked, maltreated, swindled, rejected, used, abused!" So paralysed are we.

133

The Game

Have you stood on a fairway at daybreak, waiting for your golf partner to take their shot? The air is nippy at that hour. There is the squelch of dewy grass. A steady stream of headlights snake-up from the front gate. Birds confer and call out to their clans. The trees are still emerging from the night's shadows. An odd dog barks. There is the hush of human application and aspiration. Thoughts of hot, chocolate flavoured coffee just two holes down, jig about in the pinching air. The metal face of a driver ahead, lofts an orange ball and the reverie is broken. Everyone resumes their purposeful advance towards the greens. But the opportunity comes up again. For daydreaming. Golf is like that! Punctuated with micro-skylights of zoning in and zoning out. You can be more alone in company here than any place else. It is an odd space. Your prayers are never answered. You keep hoping to come upon lost balls, but they remain in hiding. You are sure to screw up a shot right after the par, they say! Bad behaviour speaks louder on the course than anywhere else. There is a sea of unwritten rules. You must always pounce to take the putt that is conceded. The actual hit will be nothing like the practice shot. You can prepare to feel intimidated by as peripheral a thing as the adversary's fancy golf kit or her powerful drive. But there are aspects a golfer will insist, no one else who has not missed a par will know and understand. The game gets you up early. There is glamour, an eternal degree of difficulty, and an exclusivity that humans crave. It is a flourishing, prosperous world out there where rules still hold and boundaries respected. Above all, the game is an excuse to laugh at and with each other.

The Happy

Have you found yourself insistently justifying you are happy? You say things like: "But I am very happy! As long as I am happy, how does it matter? You should be happy, that's all." There is a new value in town. Happiness. Above ambition and drive and competition and struggle. It is not something you acquire or chase after or work at. It is magically accessible apparently. Given the right attitude, you can simply switch it on. There is an entire industry peddling happiness. The business of happiness is drilling holes in our pockets while chanting in our ears that if we follow their well-being bullet points, we will come to either accept the state of our lives or lose all need for a change. Be happy in other words. Are the two any different?! What is this being happy? There is the pursuit, lesson, and secret of happiness. Who is paying the bills for new designations such as that of a Happiness Minister, Happiness Centres, and Happiness Officers? Where are the realists whose lives have taught them that it is about cleaning up your act? About showing up. Sticking with it. Finishing it all. About lasting long enough to tie it up with a bow. Life is what you are married to till death does you apart. You have to learn to delay gratification. You are leaving no mark in this world if you are just happy. No wound, no greatness. No hurt, no self-expression and self-expansion. Seeking. Attempting. Failing. Learning. Now that was meant to be. It is alright to be a bit restless, unsatisfied, or hungry, therefore. These are the red flags that get humans running. When, please, did happiness become a human right? Is it not earnable, as it always was?

135

The Volvo

Have you ever started to book a Delhi-Chandigarh trip at the last minute only to find the Haryana Roadways full up? You are now care of a moustache-twirling, turban-tucking, hand-waving PunBus driver. There are shades of haughtiness in his checked shirt, thick iron bracelet, and aspirational sports shoes. He climbs into and hops off the driving seat with an authoritative spring. He drips a dry derision for the sleepy humans he carts. That's right. Most folks sleep on those buses. Volvo experience is the closest it comes to an upper-middle-class travel up north, and a true Indian will squeeze it for all it is worth. The drill is well-oiled. You book online, fetch up, cuss silently at the ten bucks charged for depositing your bag at the luggage hold below, and then lounge around until the conductor gestures. There is no great rush for cabin baggage space; people travel light on this leg. You squeeze through a padded passage and flop onto your seat, stuffing your Pepsi into the net pocket in front. Bisleri bottles are usually whimsical; they may or may not reach you. A click of ignition sets off the scratchy television that will either stream images or bellow the dialogues, never both. Following a definitive bang of the driver's window, the bus lurches out of the depot. You wake up once at the Oasis and next at the Tribune chowk. On rare occasions, you will get to chat up an interesting co-passenger. For the most, the journey is an inter-city siesta, a break from the other, a temporary reprieve where Chandigarh is the pit stop and Delhi the mad rally!

136

The Reunion

Have you entered an academy reunion at sixty years of age yet? It is lovelier than ever. More poignant; the guards are down like never before. By that age, life is done with most of you. The scars have healed, all the defending and rationalizing and anguishing behind you. There is a stoic and graceful acceptance of life's balance sheet. You skim these grey-haired people around you. They still look good, but the implants peek through smiles, the dance is a jiggle, and those voices croak even in a call to arms. This is the Boney M, Abba, Carpenters generation, nodding to notes of Summer Wine, Hey Jude, and Sweet Caroline. One wonders if they make them anymore! The last immigrants to the internet. They hug, they backslap, they punch each other…they threaten disclosures to wives of three decades! And what are the skeletons in their cupboards? Endearingly tame. Smokes, restrictions, sleeping in the classroom, and dodging riding lessons. Here, among a bunch you grew up with, you are not afraid to drop the mask. To admit that you lived by the book yet your journey brought surprises. That you put your kids first yet ended up bewildered at the outcome. That you expected an easy stepping back but are still playing the new and unfamiliar role of parenting an adult child. That for all your worldly success, you still feel like an improvising clown! The goal posts change often. Words like "individuality" and "privacy" and "personal fulfilment" are Latin. Hanging between a defined local structure and a buffeting global default, these beaming folks may appear to have lost the plot to The Hunger Games. But they hope like hell that where and how their children were raised will firmly filter out what technology relentlessly pushes at them. And Mary Hopkin croons, "Oh, my friend, we are older but no wiser, for in our hearts, the dreams are still the same…those were the days, my friends…"

137

The Kind

Have you ever killed with kindness? Your nephew is leaving home on a train journey and is fighting off a packed meal, but no. You stuff soggy tomato and cucumber sandwiches into his knapsack. He spends his journey gawking wistfully at steaming hot aloo puri on the platforms rushing by. Your hostess is buzzing around, laying the party food, and you sashay into the hectic kitchen grandly, "Can I help?" She smiles through clenched teeth as she fights you off to ease the caramel out of the mould. You are nursing a fractured nose, but there is a stream of well-wishers pouring in. You rewind and play the sequence of your fall through a Brufen-induced haze over and over. We simply have to be kind when unnecessary! We are wired to flap and cluck and coo around family and friends. Meals have ended abruptly, keys have been misplaced, and appointments missed because we cannot keep our hands to ourselves. When will we begin to respect the doer and his right to personal glory or failure? Why does everything in our lives have to be about us? My poor little beagle called Kishmish bore the brunt of our kindness recently. She conceived at the sixth attempt after running around trees with Romeo, Rocky, Bolt, Bonzo, and Mulligan respectively. An ultrasound scan, regular checks, and appropriate nutrition later, the milk of kindness became a virtual flood. Rather than trust nature and let her animal instincts guide her, I decided to take charge and be kind. Long story short, we were left with three inert pups and a hysterectomy for Kishmish. There is a time and place for everything. Even kindness.

The Joint

Have you updated your list of harmful habits to warn your kids off lately? This one is tough. Not only is it all over and everywhere, there is a perception that it is natural, part of our spiritual traditions and not habit forming. Hogwash! Cannabis or pot or marijuana or weed or *ganja* or *charas* is a mind-altering substance. It also comes in a form that is manipulated by breeders today to give the user that highest high. Young people, some as less as twelve years, are smoking up to relax, find inspiration, or merely to fit in. Most parents or teachers have no clue what weed even looks like, let alone how it is smoked in a rolled-up paper. Eye drops take care of the red eyes that come from smoking marijuana; the munchies and namkeen kids stuff their mouths with barely causes an alarm and lethargic sleepiness often gets attributed to youthful good-for-nothing laziness. Where do they get the substance? It is a phone call away. Hasher's Street in Paharganj, the neighbourhood paanwallah, dealers outside campuses, waiters in nightclubs, helpful friends. Delhi is among the top ten most stoned cities in the world. Pot has become normal, commercial, glorified and as common as soft drinks or mints or chocolates or wine. The growing demand for legalization of weed is so silent, we may get caught napping. You may want to take notice and get yourself an education if nothing else. Cannabis has medical pluses; the danger is with recreational hash thrown open to more users. The Colorado experiment with pot legalization sprung some unexpected and discouraging outcomes. No matter who is smoking up, Ranbir Kapoor or Uncle Auntie or the professionals, marijuana is known to cause short term memory losses and affect social and occupational behaviour. Lack of awareness and information about this so called "soft drug" is the biggest public health risk staring us in the face today.

The Tension

Have you ever been told not to take tension? What is with us giving and receiving so much of it? It has almost become a recreation! There's nothing much happening in our lives so let's bounce some fears off each other. What is there to inspire any confidence anyway? Rapes are raging. Economies are spluttering. Machines are relegating men. The most powerful man in the world seems to have taken leave of his senses. Is there any wonder everyone seems on edge! An Indian mother, in particular, is culturally created to emit worry twenty-four seven. No matter how hip and cheery she appears socially, dark clouds hover over her face inside her own home, supposed to be her haven. That look is a cross between a French Bulldog and a Basset Hound, mournful, wronged, long-suffering. What to do now? The offspring is out on the roads late at night with an unreachable phone. Another may be in the middle of an exam. There are applications and fee deadlines. Kids set out in the winters often without caps. They bring home unopened lunch boxes. It is quite like them not to report a safe landing even hours after leaving home. A typical Indian mum's monologue directed at her child? Are you down with a cold? Did you check in yet? Have you eaten? What did you eat? It is raining here; are you under covers where you are? Why do you keep lending your stuff to your friends? Do you have fever? Take care, alright. It is as though we are hoping for the worst. Almost as though we want our darkest fears to come true just so we are proved right. I told you so! The most satiating four words in the world.

140

The Lovebirds

Have you seen the young couples wrapped up in their bubbles at the Gardens? They remain frozen for hours together, moving barely and even then, solely for a greater angular access to the other. The hour this spectacle unfolds is about eleven in the morning, stretching well into the lunch break and beyond. I know because these are the winter months of Delhi's mellow sun, and I love walking in its forenoon snugness. The lovebirds sit cheek by jowl, whispering, gazing, peering into their mobiles occasionally. There are tears sometimes. The girl wears that feminine expression of aggrieved anguish, the boy leaning in closer as though to reassure. I try not to stare. I steal quick glances through my photochromatic frames and around my sports Bluetooth earphones. But the drama is compelling. The other day, I nearly missed my step at a desi lip-lock taking place right in my path. I looked away in haste, then flicked my eyes back just to make sure this indeed was happening in broad daylight and in public gaze. India has never before been so much in love! And because I am such an aunty, my mind goes to the parents of these lovelorn pairs. What were they told about their children's coordinates? Did they think their kids were at college or some coaching class? They look too carefree to be employed anywhere. The earth has come to a stop for them. They are entirely and wholly in the moment. I almost envy them their meditative leisure. Then my thoughts go gallivanting in another direction. They are probably emotionally illiterate. Do they know that a healthy couple love looks nothing like in the movies? That certain forms of exclusivity can be toxic. But again, this may be modern love. Caught up, yes, but convenient above everything else.

141

The Negation

Have there been times when you wanted to say no but ended up saying yes because it does not look nice?! We are programmed from childhood to accede, accommodate, and adjust. It must be our crushing numbers that makes us feel so insecure and threatened that we waste breath dressing up a plain no with vague promises, feigned illnesses, and white lies of probabilities. We will see! We will try! We will let you know! The shortest, most honest, and convenient two letter word gets stuck in our culturally constipated throats. Our inability to say no is matched only by our inability to hear no. You have to come. Alright, but please do try. Are you sure about this? We are so yellow-livered that we'd rather keep others in a state of futile expectation than relieve them of any suspense. One reason we are overweight and nursing headaches and losing our cool is because we have turned our backs on the good old "no"! Who wants to be the villain? Bollywood platelets flow after all with the white and red in our circulatory system. You are struggling with aged parents at home, a stream of house guests, and an expectant daughter, but the boss's wife has sought your talents towards an important event. You are dying to say no. You know you will die in the process of delivering. But what comes out is a saccharine, sheepish, falsely modest yes. Who wants to mess up this life's karma? People will suspect you of playing hard to get; the boss's wife will never approach you again; you will lose the attendant glory. Now the cat and mouse game begin. Deadlines fly by, unmet. Blood pressures do pole dances. Perfectionist planners make a meal of their nails. A simple no would have been the kindest environment-friendly gesture ever.

The Gift

Have you sat around your childhood heroes, watching them shuffle and suffer memory lapses? The aunties and uncles whose prowess and glamor you gawked at once. They fade now into a sepia world of silence and faraway looks. The warmth is still there, but there is a talon-like grip to their hands. You marvel at their stunning black and white pictures that come to mind. Where did that lustrous French knot go along with the Dahlia tucked in? What happened to those vibrant cravats and the buff leather shoes? You remember the Pepper Pearl and the Toffee Pearl painted nails. The pastel parasols and the elegant ear drops. The first to go is the supple skin on their hands. The dryness creeps into the necks next. The face looks jowly. They lean into their static couches. They want the fan switched off. They feel disconnected, and you wonder. Did those hands really whip up a French loaf once? Did those legs ever do the foxtrot routine that still whirls in your head? Did that muffler-wrapped throat roar those parade commands that ring in your ears? The baton, the knitting needles, the egg ball pudding, the Italian rice, the sponge roll with custard, the trips in the Ambassador car are not coming back. Ever. You turn to your parents now. They try to continue to remain assets for you. They struggle to remain relevant. Mum is still hung up on home-made pickle. Dad insists on driving his own car. But you see their confusion with their smartphones. Just getting out of the home is getting to be a chore. You fear for their dignity and safety. You want them to step back and wind down. But life is in continuing to live. It is time to return them the greatest gift they gave you. Patience!

143

The Vanity Case

Have you ever been fascinated with a deep and rectangular box that came with a handle? It had compartments. Lift the lid and there is a mirror right under. There would be a plastic tray on the top with sections for safety pins, *joodah* pins, rubber bands, and the naada *pooni*. Remove the tray and there is a long pocket all along the back for jewellery pieces or packets of *bindis*. The main compartment was a treasure chest of lipsticks and powder compacts and eyebrow pencils. There was also a round box of six or twelve tiny bottles of coloured *bindi* fluid at times. The bolder of the cases carried the foul-smelling Anne French hair removal cream too. Well, sometimes a heavy, metallic personal razor along with a packet of paper wrapped blades. Not to forget the good old, sacred *roli* thread wound around the box handle. You guessed it…the tool kit of Indian brides in the 80s. The VIP or Samsonite Vanity Case! Do brides still use those task-specific, mood-lifting little trunks? Most times in those days, you ended up with two vanity cases. The heavy armament from the parents and a perfunctory one from the parents-in-law. Well, before you got one of your own, you would have gingerly picked at an aunt's or an older cousin's treasure chest of "make-up" as "cosmetics" were called back then. From kajal cakes to Kohl pencils, from *reetha shikakai* water to hair masks, from Ponds cream to Olay regenerist…the Indian bride has come a long way. And striding there, right beside her is her groom, swinging along his Men's grooming case with aplomb. Viva la igualdad! Long live equality.

144

The Gossip

Have you caught yourself shaking your head in disapproval at idle gossip? Several times? Time and again? It is below your dignity; it is grist for other mills, the stuff made for small minds. You have better things to do. There are constructive and intellectual exploits to pursue, significant projects to be completed, goals to be met…the world needs saving. What level of pettiness would engage with human indiscretions, downfalls, and discredits? Sure, the human species has been known to stray. People cheat on their partners, they suffer professional setbacks, medical challenges pop up out of nowhere, and family impairments break hearts and spirits. But it is their personal business, all of this. What have you and I got to do with it? Oh, you know all the theory about privacy and hearsay and irresponsible tattle. But the sight of two heads close to each other, dipping ever so slightly, hands covering the mouths is a most compelling draw in social gatherings. People gravitate willy nilly to these whispered autopsies. The interest is never overt, God forbid. There is a choreography to it. You shuffle up casually. Then you flash a Madonna innocent smile. The sudden break in the conversation is your cue to close the circle. Lean a bit forward please before saying, "I don't usually like gossip. People say all kinds of things… there is always the other version after all." Your mischief making friends will nod their assent vigorously before diving back into the gore. "This is second-hand information, but apparently quantity A and quantity B have filed for divorce." A foxy cohesion comes on as the exchange progresses. There is a delicious coziness to canard. Speculation is fun; there is no audit. And you can safely step back again, shaking your head with that indulgent dismay. "People say all kinds of things!"

145

The Institution

Did you escort your precious child to a top-ranking professional school in India and leave her behind in trust and faith? You presumed the administration, the faculty, and the seniors would stand in for you. Of course, you had your peacock moment, sitting through the orientation like the proverbial cat with the cream. There were tell-tale signs, but you chose to ignore them. It had taken years of coaching classes and persistent work to break the glass ceiling of fifty-six seats in the general category. Why would you take your pink glasses off? This was it, therefore, the Promised Land, the gateway to a secure and dignified future. You would not permit the shadow of a cloud. You sashayed through the tired corridors, dismissing the jaded air in the admissions office. It piqued you that some wasted and unwashed youth lounged at the periphery of the new batch, but you averted your gaze. The claustrophobic space, the depressing rooms, the indifferent air, the greasy canteen, the distant staff, the doleful strays… you saw them all, but you chose to remember the smart library instead, the school logo at the main gate, and the green-lined pathways. On wings to ease your child's stay in the hostel, you got busy putting together the bed and bucket and bread. It was only on the flight back that you recalled clearly the college coordinator taking the mic and speaking the prophetic words, "When you return at the end of five years for the graduation, some of you will have trouble recognizing your children!" Ah, if only you had listened, you would have known how barely involved our elite schools are in the chaotic lives of their young residents.

The Consequences

How often have you absorbed and repeated community wisdom without taking a breath or blinking an eyelid? Some years ago, for instance, everybody began to swear by the smarts of the next generation. The air resounded with confident declarations that kids today are supercool. That they know exactly what they want. It doesn't matter what they do so long as they are happy. And everyone nodded vigorously. "No matter what, we have to be there for them" has been another refrain. The newest of these near-Biblical assertions is that our children must be given the space to make mistakes in addition to the freedom of choice and education. Pray why, I shall venture to ask! Can they not learn from our mistakes? We followed the markers that came from the distillation and crystallization of generations of foolhardiness. Why then should our young be free to squander precious resources, discovering what they were being told all along for free? Think about it. Societies that spout these pearls of wisdom have social security covering their young. In our country, the parents remain a child's primary support system and for life, because we are always children to our parents in these parts! Mistakes come with consequences, moreover, it is the law of nature. Who pays for the clean-up? Was this unforeseen expenditure factored into the parental charter? If so, was their assent taken? Does freedom for our young include freedom from the outcomes of their choices or actions? When did personal choice become non-negotiable? Indian parents are probably considered the world's champion narcissists, and just in case, you are privately thinking you have been a most generous and progressive one, banish that thought forthwith. There is a word for it: Delusional!

147

The Food

Where in this solar system are food demons identified and then systematically attacked? Eggs were once a cholesterol red flag; they are back to being wholesome and complete Keto delights. Remember when coconut oil was pooh-poohed and frowned upon as a high saturated fat. Any number of us are merrily downing teaspoons of raw coconut oil first thing in the morning today. Butter is in favour again after years of dry toasts. Our chapattis glisten once more with just that dab of desi ghee. Our love staple, dear dark chocolate meanwhile, it is being claimed, has the capacity to kill! And there are more new demons. Carbohydrates. Sugars. Wheat. Milk. And the new superfoods. Quinoa. Brazillian nuts. Chia seeds. Avocado. Low carb *rasbhari*. Stevia is safe, but Zevic white powder is not. What's happening? I just about got used to the goodness of flaxseeds, and pumpkins seeds are now upon us. I adored my honey when along came a dietician warning that it is not good but merely less evil than sugar. Deliver us, dear Lord, from our earthly experts! God alone knows what it costs to put food on the table and to now approach it in a perpetual state of confusion. What good is the new dietary star going to do to an already knotted stomach. Whose pockets are ringing with lucre to have us on edge at our dining tables is what I would like to know? We had a perfectly fine "*parampara*" of eating climate-friendly food. Why are mangoes and strawberries available all-round the year? It is unnatural.

The Hubris

How do you receive a friend who is bursting with self-congratulation? Perhaps they are off to a month-long trip to absorb sakuras bloom in Tokyo? It is perfectly possible they had the wildest luck with their real estate deal. They may even have just concluded a cracking nine holes at golf. So, they come expanding at you. There is a spring in their step and the faces beam, urging your participation in their seventh heaven. Smug haloes of their outsized vainglory wink and then blink. And you try! You really do. You are a good, wholesome guy. But the lips begin to thin on their own. Your heart is in place, but the liver plays hooky. What to do about this weak flesh?! The intestine squirts mini drops of acid. The more your friend squawks and preens, the narrower your eyes get. And just as they are declaring their coordinates the world's best placed, fire and ice erupt in your colon. You pull away with a weak laugh, awash with misery at your smallness by comparison. You want to be alone to beat back that pounding in your head. They are not yet done gloating. The Greek legend of Hubris is skidding on your tongue. Beware of the wrath of the gods, you want to warn them. But then the cloud of envy rips, and you pause to ask yourself, *would you rather be them?* Of course, not. In the interest of public health, however, we could certainly afford to crow a bit less.

149

The Energy

Have you noticed how greatly in love India is in these trying times? It is as though we have decided to make the most of peace and food and water and green cover while it lasts. Couples abound. Dating apps make a killing. Teenagers are almost feverish, and young adults are riding a maelstrom of breakups. Some seniors seem to have quietly caught the bug too, but let's first talk of the country's famously large youth band. One dimly recalls a figure called Devdas who drowned his pain in vice and alcohol, and not for one moment is that the suggested escape. But what is the modus operandi today to deal with the emotional rejection and fatigue that invariably comes at the end of the honeymoon phase of every romantic relationship? Another partner? Another beginning? And another split. If there is one energy that is sucking dry India's productive young, it is this epidemic of the red roses. The wo/man hours, the money, the life force lost is heart-breaking. Call an Indian youth, and s/he will be nursing his heart, hunched over WhatsApp or fighting a fog of depression. When and if the healing comes, it brings numbness or the cruelty of cynicism. Where is Elon Reeve Musk? Do his eyes not glint at the oodles of love energy the subcontinent is in the process of churning out? The flaming output could fire the engines of his Mission Mars. It would also mop up the aridity India's emotional gluttony seems to leave behind. "At least it was *my* choice!" I have been reminded by a young friend.

150

The Rush

What is it with us women and golf? Do men too fight internal battles during a game? My guess is they keep it all in while we keep up a nonstop chatter of self-recrimination across every single hole right until the end of the game. It begins at the tee off, this expression of self-doubt and apprehension at what is about to come. The speaker will usually claim a long gap gone without playing while the listener, she will insist, has been playing "so regularly." The rationalizing, the justifying, the apologizing… there is a veritable fest. You want to focus on keeping your rebellious head down, on keeping the weight on your left foot, on coming down with speed under the ball, but you find yourself cooing sounds of assurance to your golf buddy. It is alright; everyone has a bad day at golf, you insist. Don't be so angry at yourself; this is not a matter of life or death. But the pity party persists. Oh, that tree should not have been there! Oh, I am so sorry I messed up that fairway stroke! Oh, what is happening to me today; only yesterday, I scored a par on this very hole. Golf exposes and tests the players like no other game. It is a private battle in public eye. Not just your skill set but your beliefs, your character, your potential for future partnerships… it is all on display. At the bottom of muffed drives, missed putts, and duff lofts are the three sterling commandments of decent golf. Own your bad game. Laugh at yourself. And let it go. Hell, it is only a game; you are still you. And lady, do not rush!

VI

OPEN SECRET

151

The Grandparents

Have you wondered at the first word that pops into your head at the mere mention of a grandmother? It is "*Nani*." That is how it is. The ideal grandmother. The picture made up of our cultural experiences, that person we associate with the most generous version of unconditional love is usually the mother of your mother. She is indulgent to a fault. She is your child's adjutant, their back-up force, their insurance against your parenting! Chocolates, riotous hair accessories, Doy animal-shaped soaps, gallons of Frooti, and dozens of bows and tassels on showy kid clothes. A *nani* is sure to be lurking somewhere, clutching her heart and purse. Hello, but where is the *dadi*? The father's mother has her place; she sits on a slightly elevated ledge, on pillars of affectionate distance, and a tentative respect. Her presence is real and non-negotiable. Regular check-ins take place at her door, but something about the family dynamics prevents her from practicing the *nani's* brand of enmeshment. That's how it used to be since times immemorial. But like all else, these subsystems are shifting. Some grandparents are getting to parent their grandkids. There are others who would like their own space and time. With some young parents, it is a matter of their self-sufficiency that they not expect their babies to be raised by their parents. It is hard at times to tell one from the other. Grandparents retire later, are fitter, and some go bustling about, striking off their own bucket-lists. Below these surface shifts are the grandkids who, thankfully, continue to be overfed and told stories of Kaju, the monkey!

The Dead

Do you crave being alone with yourself in these times of ruthless invasion of your person? There is no hiding! If you switch off your double blue tick on WhatsApp, they will cross-check on Facebook. Should that prove futile, they will ferret you out on Twitter or Instagram. It is airless, this omnipresent virtual closeness. There are moments you want to wear your doomsday face without anyone oozing concern, "Is everything OK?" There are weeks that you need to ride with your head down. What? No posts lately? Is all well, your friends are sure to wonder. My generation are the immigrants to this constant glare. How about our kids, the natives? No wonder they periodically want to hide, go away to the mountains. Solitude is, after all, oxygen to self-repair. Our need for me-time is as organic as our sociability. But we have invented new stress triggers for ourselves. No response to your group message is a slur. Benefit of a doubt is as rare online as it is in the physical world. Heaven help you if you do not respond to a call from a family member! Within minutes, five other hapless folks in your immediate radius will have been contacted as to your likely whereabouts. Speculations are in a specific order. You are in an accident! You have been kidnapped by the Naxalite! The Martians have grabbed you! There are only two ways to be today. You are either online or dead!

153

The Memories

Have you tried this exercise ever? In the middle of an action or an event or a happening you are involved in, have you taken a step back to see the colour and shape of the memory you are creating? The moment is flowing by even as you are living it, but it is never truly gone. It lives on in our hearts and minds, causing us pleasure or pain ahead. Every living moment of our lives, we craft our recollections! Creating vignettes that add up to the sum total of what we become. Our physical health, our basal facial expression, the weight of our being is made up of this hark-back; never mind how much we are told not to look behind. Regret, shame, and disappointment are cancerous emotions. They manifest in strange, psychosomatic symptoms. Some events are beyond our control. Accidents happen. The market crashes. Earthquakes hit. But there is our daily communication with our immediate ecosystem that we fashion. The default setting is one of preoccupation and that is fine because there are deadlines and appointments and functions to be dealt with. But right there, in this hectic maze are opportunities to connect. And if there is this link, can we help ourselves just watching what we are so busy creating with our words and thoughts and body? Memories. Or mammaries in Hinglish!

The Struggle

Have you been too ready to console, quick to reassure, instant with the band-aid? We are like that only. It must be our history of being invaded by one marauder after another. They came lusting for the golden bird, the spices and muslin, and doe-eyed women. It must have hurt, the plundering and taking by force. It would have left behind festering souls that could bear no more to see one more cry of anguish. Perhaps we busied ourselves hushing, shushing, and puch-puching! There, there, stop it now. Do other cultures practice our brand of invasive consoling? We take over. We can't bear to see another bawl. One wonders if it is the soother's own discomfort, they want to stop by moving in to manage grief and struggle. Everyone without exception will find themselves in testing waters where they will have to call upon their deepest, hidden, and highly personal resources to swim across treachery. Fortunately, humans come wired for survival and self-direction. The most respectful and effective gesture would be to give the fighter space to stew and surface. And applaud furiously when they do. Crowding does nothing but cuts into their personal autonomy and sets off dangerous feelings of failing fatigue. Humans thrive on beating back challenges. There is something primal in us that will find ways to survive. We come designed for self-repair. If only our cultural memory would permit us room for movement!

155

The Peers

Do you associate peer pressure with the young? Truth be told, we are all driven by it to varying degrees. Remember that time common sense told you there were enough sarees in your stock, but all around, there was a babble about the terrific indigo prints at *Gamthi*. You went scurrying, terrified of missing out. Enough had been said by family as to your singularly lacklustre stove skills, but everyone was making the life-transforming purchase of this Morris Oven. Never one to be left behind, you carefully considered between ivory and beige shades, never mind the food warming role you relegated the oven to thereafter. You were abreast with peers! Then tomato prices fell across the Doaba belt. Skilled homemakers went flocking to the kitchen, rolling out one bottle after another of thick tomato puree. The air resounded with self-congratulation on their clever resource management. You imagined a wistful look in your husband's eyes and that sent you scrambling to the wholesale tomato market. Then this one particular garden would glow on the social media, lush and picture-book pretty. And of course, you had to have that arched bamboo door, the brightly painted tyre pots, the imitation wicket fence, and the useless wrought iron chairs, painted just that antique green. That one time when you were moving into a new house, and short on days, just waiting to open up and get comfortable, but a peer pointed out, "Aren't you renovating a bit?" You promptly went back and made peace with your suitcases two more months. Peer pressure keeps us in check and out of harm's way. We could easily go off track. As it is, we manage to stand out even amidst the peer pressure, and that is another one of those…the peer pressures!

156
The Gawd

Have you realized that the one-to-one phenomenon is a thing of the past? No twosome is by themselves anymore. There is a constant third. The digital being. It is creepy. You will be delivering a careful and even-voiced sermon to your scruffy youngster, and he will respond in an unfamiliar tenor. Unknown to you, his friend is participating in your mother-son engagement via WhatsApp! The digital has become Gawd, omnipresent, omnipotent, omniscient. The forum is redefining us in ways unexpected. You have sent your pictures to a good friend; they in turn share it with their good friend…a circularity that would not normally take place in the physical world. Our brains have acquired an external drive, our phones. You have missed a class? Just have someone grab the board and notebook content. You are a guest at an event, and the decor is divine. Out comes the camera, swoosh, swish, snap. No need for polite permission or pleasant enquiries. You are in a royal sulk with your partner, but a parent is on hand for emotional tutoring. Homes, bedrooms, vanity rooms, washrooms, boardrooms, the machine is in attendance. Teenagers speak with the Googled brand of certainty and authority their grandparents associated with fathers, bosses, and religious heads. The future is here! You and I with our extended third, the smartphone. It just needs to go subdermal next. One chip under the skin, and you will never be alone, even between calls and texts. Ever. Fancy that!

157

The Ritual

Do you harbour memories of rituals at home you chafed at when young? They just did not seem to make sense. You dismissed them at times as inferior humbug of your third-world culture. Why did a visitor, for instance, have to be pressed with a glass of water just as he placed foot into your home? Potable water would have been a precious resource, and people once walked or rode animals to their destinations. With no roadside restaurants and pet water bottles yet to come, the arriving humanity would have been dehydrated?! A prompt serving of water would have made ample sense! It used to be a common practice for the family elders to press some money at loved ones departing from home. Mock resistance involving two people pushing and pulling at a wad of currency even today is a familiar sight in many northern homes. One could surmise that travellers once carried their cash deep inside their luggage. The departure allowance stayed accessible and handy for unexpected surprises on their journey. It also encouraged future visits! Speaking of travels, there was the curd and sugar potion saved for the absolute last goodbye. The car ignition would have come to life as one junior scampered around with a bowl while family made faces at Grandma's insistence on the offending spoonful. No one remembered to mention the calming and restorative properties of the potion. Having been repeated mechanically over generations, many of these meaningful rituals have come to be viewed as symptoms of a dense, unwieldy, and apologetic way of life.

The Nutrition

Who ever said humans are creatures of reason and logic? We are quivering masses of welling eyes and undulating bosoms. We thrive on emotions, the grammar built on memories of tastes and sounds and tactile recollections. Oh, the sickly-sweet pungency of Pachmarhi's grape-like "*Mahua*" and how it transports me to that Queen of the Satpuras. There amidst the hills and the vales, we would grind the *imli* tree leaves under our milk molars; my mouth floods, forty-five years later, at the raw crunch of the green "*kairi*." It will remain with me for as long as forever, the juiciness of those black Lantana berries and the funky odour of its flowers. How do you forget the knotty weave of the "*amarbel*," the nutty sharpness of "*chironji*," and the intricacy of Pachmarhi's "ferns"? These are associated with the idea of home, of being cherished, of being cared for. Any wonder that we continue to press home-made pickles and savouries and sweets on family in transit. Our carefully sealed packets are substitutes for our presence. One hug in rural Punjab from a family elder does more for me than all the calcium and vitamin supply in my medicine dispenser. There it is in that envelope of eager arms, the smell of white butter and hay and smoke and fuel cakes and the integrity of honest to goodness labour. Give us this day, dear lord, our *besan* ladoo, aata *pinnis, methi papdis, till* ke ladoo, peanut *chirwa*, golden *murrukus*, and chocolate fudge. Sprinkle on the men though, a little bit amnesia over the pull of their childhood nourishment!

159

The Beverage

Have you secretly known that the fine life is wasted on you? Take wine, for instance. With your eyes shut, you probably couldn't tell red from white. And if you did recognize the sweeter notes of one over the other, you'd be hard put to pin the make. But we are wining away anyway. The dining fare is butter *naan* and *shahi paneer*, but the beverage on offer is incongruously wine! There is a choice, but you have no clue which goes better with *dal makhani*. Earthy or fruity? It is not a taste you have grown up with. You play safe and decline, a nagging inadequacy sniffing at you. It is no different at an evening with friends. The host offers, "I have some home-made wine. Try some; you will like it!" When he circulates back at you, wanting feedback, you stretch your lips, baring sugary teeth, the voice weak. "Very nice!" It is syrupy. There is a rich aftertaste. You don't want to finish it. The husband's antenna is dead to your pleas to share please, so you soldier on grimly, forcing images of cough syrup out of your head. Now *chai* and *lassi* you know—you have it pat down. Dhabba or Nonsuch? Brewed or boiled? All-nighter or wake up? Farm smoky or processed? But champagne or beer or wine…the cost-benefit analysis is sure to swing negative. Your palette of taste just does not have the shades or words enough. It is an import, just like the Cheese platter. You have grown up besides, watching women down anything faintly alcoholic in tumblers of steel. Out of respect, you see.

160
The Review

Do you have an elder at home who appears to have zoned out? They surface in spurts for meals and TV. Also, for medicines, multiple tablets, at times numbering twenty plus. It is a familiar scenario in many homes today. Elderly care shuffles along despite a fundamental care and concern. New medical problems arise, quick fixes are patched on, and it is back to business. Family is busy even though there are a lot of enquiries, and second, third, fourth opinions are sought. What sneak past unnoticed are consistent reviews, and there are reasons. Our elderly shift base from one child to another, each of whom feels they know what is best for their parents! Consensus on the course of action takes time, not least of all being the senior's own style of personal management. Yes, of course, they have their own home, but in their increasingly frail state, they are perhaps unable to construct a sustainable medical protocol for themselves. So, there you have these loved elders, ingesting a toxic cocktail of ill-matched medications that feed on the scraps of life force left in them. Every one of us is getting there sooner or later. Given the pragmatic and self-absorbed ecoshphere today, the seniors would do best to keep their net-worth high right until the end. Even if they are babysitting, don't be in a hurry to hand over the keys yet, and for heaven's sake, let's keep all the review appointments.

The Debt

Has it dawned yet that India is vying for the crown of the world's most sleep deprived nation? We are not there yet, but the signs are everywhere. People are just not shutting down anymore. The young have rejected regular hours both in principle and practice. They refuse to commit to the good old timetable. They treat their bodies like Public Transport Carriers. Keep running until dry, then flop by the wayside for recovery, not too picky about the spot or surface. The zombies stumble around with baggy eyes, hyper-aroused on screen-fare, and me-time. They add fuel to the fire by dunking black coffee on insomnia. Day and night are no more antonyms. The small red fridge in the dining hall swings on its hinges through the night. It has become cool to roam the roads for "chai" at two or three am, facilitated by the 24/7 stores and all-night dhabas. And not just the BPO industry, take the media, advertising, or corporates, there is no defined pack-up time. Pulling an all-nighter is an acceptable synonym for creative crushing output! There was a nightly routine once. Dinner, Chitrahaar or Krishi Darshan, a glass of hot milk, toothbrush, and lights out. The landscape today is littered with professionals snoring around half-crooked reading glasses perched on their noses in bed; there are fatigued bodies wrapped awkwardly around books; necks get more and more angular peering at Amazon Prime screens on bed tables. From eight hours in 1942, the average norm has slipped to 6.8 hours. Homes no longer get swept and dusted and mopped in one go. Someone is always asleep behind closed doors at all hours of the day. What's your sleep debt?

162

The Alliance

id you know that the biggest waste on earth is a Lutyen's bungalow that has not seen a wedding? It is criminal to not have flogged all that acreage for at least a "*roka*" or a "*sangeet*." There is just one tiny problem. The chief artists, the eligible singles play spoilsport, baulking a bit much, heels dug in, issuing statements like, "Why would I marry to save you a couple of lakhs rental?" Or "It is horrible how parents can mount such a spectacle just so two people can have sex." The landscape of love has transformed beyond recognition. It used to be marriage, love, then baby carriage. The order is highly unpredictable today. Fortunately, the subcontinent seems to have found a happy compromise in self-arranged alliances. First comes compatibility, then comes the family trooping in, and voila, we have the happy makings. Or do we? What would explain the serial break-ups and second weddings in that case? Given the freedom of choice, young people ought to give better success rate than the generations that were merely bundled and packed off to new homes. But media images of the successful and gorgeous Katrina Kaif admitting to falling apart over her break-up with Ranbir Kapoor speak otherwise. Given women empowerment and gender equality, one would have expected Kaif to better negotiate the treacherous waters of love? Lord Byron famously said two hundred years ago, "Man's love is of man's life a thing apart, 'Tis woman's whole existence." Not much seems to have changed since. Kaif's 2019 checklist leads with a boyfriend! And if the race is to catch up with Priyanka, Deepika, and Anushka, wouldn't it save time and health and the system to, well, arrange one?!

The Potential

Have you noticed how we barely, hardly, warm up in our country before any physical performance? It must be the lack of resources. We don't have enough to waste on foreplay; just cut to the core. Our notion of the build-up is not educated by any detail of human physiology or nutritional protocol or performance psychology. The indigenous formula is simple. "Don't be a sissy; stick it out, you shirker; now get on with it!" So, you have cycling groups flashing the fanciest lights and humming on pricey gears, but no warm up. The bunch bolts like bullets at flag off, but there's no spacing. Our revered classical dancers are no better. Peek into the green room before the dancer is announced; they'll be pirouetting and striking the floor with their feet mostly to test that their attire is secure. A full-fledged class in preparation for a ballet performance is not our way! We are "*rrappa* ready" always. Watch us dive into the pool, tee off on the course, trot off on the cross-country run…all at a clip and with just the pretence of a warm up, not even a limbering up. Just a haphazard throwing of the limbs around and oh, that jerking of the shoulders. The most ambitious will throw their hands up and keel over to grasp at their toes. And whoever heard of public speakers discharging a voice warm up before they take to the microphone? We just launch. Outcomes shall be willed via sound and fury. Why bother to potentiate when we can be just as happy with the potential?!

The Scent

Are you out of sorts with perfumes as you have known them? Not in terms of breaking into a hive or a sneezing fit, but in being ambivalent towards them. What is this smell of spring, for instance? Or aroma of the peony? Sensual musk anyone? Be the most luxurious of international brands, the Indian weather reduces them all to one common indistinguishable assault, the top notes being sweat and dust. There has been this aspirational mystique around good perfume, parfum, and eau de toilette. Take the names, for instance. Cool water, Boss, Nautica Blue, Creed, Nina Ricci, Marc Jacobs, Chanel. And their attributes? Floral, forest blend, fruity, heady, herbaceous, velvety, spicy, mossy, leafy. One reads evocative passages and watches tantalizing film shots of a sniff that ensnares, but in life, this side of the equator, the celebrated smells do nothing for the wearer and the sufferer. Have you inhaled anything worse than the whip of a foreign fragrance gone rancid with daily living in desi spaces? The Deodorant-come-lately fever takes public suffocation a step further. Fragrances ought to be rooted in cultural poignance and wistfulness. The draught of vanilla takes me nowhere. Give me the waft and flurry of *nargis*, *gulab*, jasmine, sandalwood…the breath and trace of pepper and cardamom!

165

The Twin

Are you a split personality? God forbid. But there is a social media "you" and the "real" you. How close are the two? What is factual? You or the world's perception of you. Quite unintentionally, you are creating this digital 'you' that people receive without the filters that operate in the physical world. You post a couple of fun pictures of a golf game with buddies. Done consistently, they present you as a better golfer than you actually are! The context and physical veracity are missing from these online interactions. You manage a selfie one day with Smriti Irani, the MP, at the Craft Emporium, and lo and behold, an invite to the Textiles Convention follows. Someone presumes your association is professional. A share of your book launch may be interpreted as the showcasing of a bestseller. There is this one-way invincibility to what we post on our various social accounts, an unguided missile out there once shared. The young, in particular, paint false images of themselves, posing against their father's SUV or an uncle's rifle or the violent lyrics of a rap song. What would appear as harmless and age-appropriate pranks outside of the internet may lead to job offers withdrawn, matrimonial prospects lost, and in some cases, incarceration. We are co-creating our Frankenstein twin every time we post. You could be Adam or the fallen Angel or somewhere in between, but as to where precisely, there's no knowing for a fact anymore.

The Art

How do you react when presented with a work of art? Are you shaken, stirred, or just a tiny bit intimidated? Say you are not a museum person—many are not enthused at the idea of shuffling from one panel to another—but you have been snared into the visit by your sight-seeing guests. You gather yourself and face the certified masterpiece. The brain shifts into lower gear; you fear that you are not quite getting it. You dive into your heart and plumb your mind and senses, in desperation. You are not sure what it is supposed to do to you. The figure, the landscape, the brush strokes, the overall effect, the detailing. You stare. Then you take half a step back, the head tilting a degree or two, the right forefinger and thump creep up and cup your chin, and you swivel and steal a quick glance around. Other viewers seem to radiate sensitivity. You are certain they are seeing something invaluable on the canvas. The brows begin to knit now, eyes narrowing to get at the painter's intention. What did he want to say? Artists don't necessarily create art for money or fame. They have a need to express, connect, and leave behind a ripple, at the very least. Bright blobs or drab dabs, if the art reaches out of the frame to touch you, it is great, and we are not alone. Does it…speak to you?

167

The Name

Why do we baptize our pets with anglicized names? Fluffy, Candy, Buster, Cocoa, Bruno. Not Lali, but Lyka. Not Bhalu, but Brut. Not Kaalu, but Pepper. Not Bhura, but Biscuit. Even the receptionist at the vet's will jump if you answer his routine query with a name like Moti or Heera or Piloo. One wonders as to what makes Apple and Misty more acceptable than Kaaju or Kishmish? Sure, the name ought to be pithy, easy on both the tongue and the ears. But Deepa or Lata or Shiv or Uday would risk offending a namesake biped in the radius. Sammy, moreover, sounds hipper than Shyam. It has to be our foreign fixation surely! Our domestic pet breeds are international, you see. Picture a Dalmatian named Ashok. Or a Golden Retriever who answers to Sushant. Oh no! Newton and Caesar and Apollo or Napoleon are alright, but most certainly not Drona or Swamy or Ramanujan or Patanjali. It would be blasphemous! Moreover, the dogs only understand English. Mac fetch. Errol stay. Mulligan beg. Arrow roll. Nandi, the dachshund, is a rarity! Fancy Purushottam, the Alsatian, and Lavanya, the Beagle. It's a wonder this abysmal symptom of Colonial Imperialism has not come in for abolition by the nationalist powers that be. Until that inevitability comes about, let every dog have his day!

168

The Capital

Have you dreaded coming to Delhi only to end up miserable having to leave the city eventually? Did someone in your vicinity express incredulity that you would want to hang on in the capital city "for the heck of it"? Are you hard put to explain your love for the alleged-rape capital of the world; this conglomerate of people with sour lemon faces and self-important airs? The know-alls and the cynics; the measuring eyes and their wary doff to hierarchy. This is the national city of food chains folks, from the Tiger down to the monkey; everybody knows where they come in, but they will masquerade a step higher anyway. There is a self-assuredness that comes from the proximity to power, never mind how removed. It is a city that panders to the privileged, but the rest have their own little bubbles in spaces such as outside the Sai Baba Temple or around the bushes in the Garden of Five Senses or under the Moolchand Flyover. Delhi is to India what a kitchen is to your home. Would you stay away from the cookhouse? The "Khichdi," the "masalas," the sustenance, and the action is all around the gas range. Delhi has it all: the pantry of goods and services and products and facilities. There is a certain satiety in just knowing it is on hand. You may sample, but a few, be allergic to most and be in absentia when the kitchen gets too hot, but home after all is where the hearth is! This city of aspirations, strife, and expediency, this Washington of Asia, this National Capital Region, this shot at grandeur and history, the city of my love, Delhi.

169

The Lighting

Have you exercised strategic brilliance in placing the lighting just so in your drawing room? It reflects off the brass tastefully, nullifying the overzealous "*peetaambari*." That crack in the onyx candle holder…it is as good as new in the shadows. The craft lamps cast pools of character over the paintings, lending them depth and dimensions. The Belgian carpet is richer in semi-darkness, the tiniest of tucked frays escaping notice. Your booty of artificial flowers is almost natural in the low-light kindness. This cowl of compassion is your creation. You play with wattage and angles for that arty, cosy, rich look so as to calm. The pretty palms in tasteful pots stand guard over an odd patch on the wall. Sheer flutters over the bay windows lend glamour and a subdued promise. Everything and everyone looks filtered, softer, better-looking. You relax in this cocoon you have ensconced your guests in. The cocktails look dressy and the snacks fetching, in their half-lit shapes and textures. One piano rendition after another floats, and you begin to sit back. A sudden stir. There is a busy flutter. The husband looms, head craned at the various beverages on the tray. He squints, quickly skips over, and snaps on all the switches along the wall. Impatient stabs, every one of them. The illusion shatters, and you sit there feeling utterly and absolutely denuded.

The Wallet

Have you, dear lady, ever plucked money out of your husband's wallet without his knowledge? It happens more than we think. The poignancy lies not in the act but in there being a need to do so. Patriarchy is spoken most times in terms of bigger issues like the rape culture or slut shaming or gender stereotypes, but there are tinier tell-tale symptoms of a system that places one gender higher in position, power, and privilege. Who amongst us has not grown up with a subconscious cultural debris of the archetypal Indian housewife? On the first day of every month, her husband places a specific wad of money on her palm, and she administers the home affairs on that budget. It caters to the basal, the necessary, and the sufficient expenditure in a typical Indian home. It leaves out any scope for an occasional retail therapy, some amount of giving to the wife's family, relationships she might wish to nurture, independent of her husband. And forget about any of her personal growth; married life ought to be enough. It is acceptable for him to live up to his role of a potent, productive community member, but she ought to derive satisfaction by proxy. Well, she was a full-fledged person before she joined forces with him. She has her share of give and take to honour and no personal source of income to fund those very human negotiations with. And so, she gets inventive! Tiny lies. Quick swipes. Stowing in safe spaces, cash deposits with a close neighbour or a sister. Under-reporting the grocery. Ah, it is fragile, this thing called human dignity, this legacy of self-worth we inherit and then mash up.

The Return

Have you heard the imperceptible chink of parental hearts breaking lately? Those love-soaked bosoms of Indian moms and dads, in particular. That species that Quora strings vilify as the world's most repressive, authoritarian, and rigid. That interfering, hovering, controlling community that treats their children as extensions of themselves, as trophies, as proxies to live their dreams through. That emotionally abusive, unfulfilled, incessantly attentive piece of humanity that claims it only wants their children to be happy but "their way." Psychology, sociology, media, law, the airwaves are chock-a-block today with versions of poor parenting. Guilty as charged, modern Indian parents do not stand a chance unless they push aside the mountains of blame and guilt being dumped on them and speak up. What were they thinking? Well, most Indian parents are middle-class, regular-looking folks and citizens of a schizophrenic democracy. No great riches, no stunning looks, no consistent returns on taxes. The two things that seem within reach to them are getting their children skills and an education. They gather themselves, therefore; they hunker down and stake it all on their precious progeny, putting them first and always. They tell themselves they are giving their offspring the best shot at a life of dignity and plenty. But the young? Their Pied Piper sits elsewhere, in an internet nebula of globally articulated goals and gains. Freedom of choice! Happiness above all else! Everything or nothing! This generation that has had the most "progressive" parenting in the history of India looks like giving the lowest percentage all-inclusive return on assets. Exit poll of the "nirodh" generation's parenting, anyone?

172
The Plan

Have you caught yourself voicing plans you know you are never going to execute? It happens to be our default setting! You have, for instance, always visualized yourself running an Italian Restaurant. You know you have an eye for beauty and craft, and you fancy yourself in a knick-knack store for folks of good taste. Perhaps you have been lauded on multiple occasions for your ability to connect with the audience, and you begin to see yourself as a life coach. They are pipe dreams mostly, these wistful ruminations, quite like the New Year resolutions that are grandly declared only to sink into the soft bed of the inertia that follows. There is this delusion we all nurture that we have plenty of time. It's all going to happen some day when everything is just so. We apparently have an eternity ahead. The truth is that all great accomplishments were built on a series of bite-sized shuffles forward. Nothing dramatic, nothing overnight, just the drudgery of daily discipline. Marathons are run a few kilometres at a time. Bestsellers get written a paragraph at a time. Reputations are built an achievement at a time. But what if inspiration comes knocking like Lakshmi on Diwali night? Better to sit tight, no! After all, we have it in us; it is just a matter of time. Truth be told, thinking about doing something is more tiring than just going ahead and doing it.

The Taste

Have you ever worn a dress that did not meet your exacting standards but was bought very fondly by a loved one? Maybe dear husband got you a *bandhani* suit the colour of a MIG 29? It could be that a mother brought up in the deserts of Rajasthan can't help buying gigantic floral prints for you! Or a child, with just enough money, brings home a bag with golden studs. But you are a lady of impeccable taste. You feel and breathe only around the colours and textures of England. The English is superior on the subcontinent's cultural scale. Classy is subdued. Classy is colourless. Classy is minimal. It has to be just so for you to allow it within a foot of you. You wouldn't be seen dead in a bright hue unless it is the tint of French wine or Italian celeste or rosado of Spain. Anything other than the Indian palette of violent purples and anguished oranges and hungry greens. There is this strange Brahminism of "taste," and mostly amongst women. Beige is superior to orange. Indigo rates higher than peacock blue. Silver grey beats gaajari. Parrot green and magenta and *Phirozi* blue are nearing extinction. The burden of keeping alive *Moongia* and *Kathhai* is on the turbaned shoulders of a particular community. And what happens to the Hindu custom of red on Sunday, yellow on Monday, blue on Friday etc. Small mercy that the performing arts in India have not gone neutered yet. Fancy watching a Bharatanatyam recital in pale peach or a Kathak performance in fading mauve. Whither, our true colours?

The Respect

Have you heard it said that Indians lack the free spirit and irreverence needed to invent? That they do not question enough. That they are brought up to respect age and authority. That they expect the collective to look after their interests. It is not in them to challenge the status quo unless pushed by a sense of self-preservation. There will, therefore, be a famine of patents this side of the world. Intellectual property will remain an alien concept. We shall be plagued by corruption and cronyism and that signature tendency to crawl! No denying that India's servile history and a deep-seated insecurity has turned us into "annoying jugaadoos," but well, how far has its culture of disrespect taken the other hemisphere? Their streets hum with the irreverence of feral kids. At the beck and call of their children, parents are no longer presumed to know what is best for their gen-next. Popular culture depicts them as buffoons, Indian comics too have taken that cue and are busily pulling down uncles and aunties from their once authoritative pegs. Live for now. If it feels good, just do it. Delayed gratification is an ancient dictum today. So, there you have it. No nagging community nor culture, so no holding up of moral values and responsibility. There was a polite friendliness Indian adults were once greeted with by their young. Today, their evasive eyes say, "Earn our respect, old fogie. It is not enough that you have negotiated survival longer."

175

The Waste

Have you realized yet what a ride higher education is taking us for? It is a nightmare, a herculean project, quite heart-breaking, this formula to break the glass ceiling of admissions. Given that the kid does feature on the main list, there follow years of family investment of emotional and financial and physical nature. But the associated hope and sense of pride keeps everyone going. Many grandparents pitch in with the fees; they are so besides themselves with joy to see the next generation on the cusp of flowering. Having expended themselves on preparing for these highly competitive examinations, our children bumble along meanwhile, handling their apathetic elite school administration and an environment of insecure envy. Come graduation day, and the kith and kin troop out in their ceremonials, the social media buzzing with pictorial updates. It touches you, the naive notion oozing off these perfect frames that now on, life's compass is in place and the path cleared. Then the grind begins. The heart-in-mouth process of placements. The college loan instalments. The investment involved in setting up at the new place of work. The newly-minted, now slightly mollified graduates fetch up at their offices. The jaded employers give the newbies an up and down before barking an order over their shoulders, "Get to work on making them unlearn everything they learnt at school. It will take time, but we have to start afresh. What a waste of our money!"

The Sibling

Have you had to clarify often if the sister you are referring to is real or cousin? First or second cousin? Which side of the family? Maternal or paternal? There is that bemused furrowing of the brows, nearly vexatious. "He is your real brother? Really? Real brother?" The exclamations then snowball. Oh, but you look so different. What's your age difference? Siblings can be poles apart. At times, the cousins are more similar, growing up. But it is poignant, this relationship, of your childhood. In a room full of people, two siblings can be sniggering at the inside jokes while the rest look on in annoyance. The stories do not change. They will be retold a million times and chuckled over again and again. One will begin an anecdote and the other is sure to snatch the thread and complete it. There is a playful sweetness to these shared memories. The DNA peeps through in a hundred ways. Physicality, habits, life's priorities, one's attitude towards living and the world. The older they get, the greater the intensity with which nostalgia strikes. The childhood rivalry is forgotten. Without saying it, they know… they know the time left together is running out. Immortality is not here yet despite Elon Musk. There is a determined return to their shared roots, the food, the traditions at home. Surprisingly so, it must be a survival instinct, the charm holds true only when applied to your own siblings, not your spouse's!

The Start-up

Has your child ditched the traditional employment track in favour of launching a start-up? Heartfelt sympathies on the rollercoaster stretching ahead. Strap up, please, store your dreams and plans in the cabin overhead and grip the armrests. The oxygen mask will drop often, grab at it and conserve yourself. There is no blue book for this flight; you will be improvising as you go along. Stay calm. Your world is about to change. What a sight you are, a baby boomer who believed one was either a doctor or an engineer or an abject failure! The spin shows miles away as you wrap your head around this unfolding drama. The toughest question you dread having to answer will be "What does she do?" You are not sure yourself since the model seems to evolve as you go along. That's it. Harder still to be rendered completely irrelevant by your youngster's ambition. You have nothing to offer: no perspective, no advice, no insight. You stand by as a mentor sitting in the Silicon Valley, the Start Up Bibles, and a few friends of the same feather cast their spell on your precious child. She babbles a foreign language of words such as scale up, organic search engine optimization, and product validation. It will feel like an eternal wait. But pat yourself on the back! You will be the first generation of Indian middle-class parents to have box seats to this chaotic, controversial but the coolest new phenomenon of the start-ups. May the kids prove their families wrong!

178

The Uniform

What goes through your head when you see a uniform? You see the crisp crease, perhaps not the years and toil it took to get to wear it. You see the sharp brocade, not the painstaking care and pride of place the garment receives in the home of the wearer. You register the shiny reflections on the stars and buttons but do not associate it with that singular brand of commitment. There is the glory of a community pact, an unsaid promise of integrity, an irrevocable obligation to risk life and limb, if need be, in that ensemble. An infinite liability lies behind those conforming regimentals. The years don't matter; ten or twenty or thirty-nine, you honour those threads with every fibre of your being while the privilege of wearing them lasts. Many a cusp, many a squall shall cross you, but you get up, strap up, and fetch up in them trappings. You steel yourself. Oh, you stay the course for the bagpipers you march to, come from all over the country. Your course-mates wave you on and up the ladder with an esprit de corps. Your staff gives immeasurably of their time and energy and loyalty. Your family is hugely invested in the regalia. It truly is an exclusive legacy, this readiness for a call to arms. Today, one such uniform shall be hung up for one last time. But somewhere not far off, a brand-new kit is being brassoed. Long live the uniform and the world around it!

179

The Amoral

Have your millennials begun talking of dumping marriage yet? They are probably saying the institution is unnecessary and patriarchal and limiting and dated. Co-habitation is perhaps being spoken of in whispers as a strong alternative. As per data, at least twenty-five percent of American adults today are living together without being married. It is a lifestyle template knocking at several other nationalities including those with a history of strong social sanctions, such as India. There are a few basic premises involved here. Women empowerment leads women to assume they must be entirely self-sufficient financially before biting the dust. Married life appears dusty, judging by what they see of the survival-driven partnership of their parents. It looks nothing like the idea of romance floated by cards from Archies or King Khan's *Kuch Kuch Hota Hai* eyes. What was once known as immorality is today called amorality, given that sexuality has been divested of any accountability or responsibility. There is no right or wrong. Young people are determined to be who they think they are and not who they are expected to be. There is a peculiar and progressive naivety free floating amongst us. Anything and everything gets rewarded with a parade in the name of liberal humanism. We are treading treacherous depths with the sexual revolution in India made more dangerous by the parental lack of vocabulary to refute the wave. What, for instance, did the West gain from the hipster, free love epoch other than an STD epidemic, unwed pregnancies, abortions, a spike in divorce rate, and heartbreaks all around? This is not just about being religious or conservative or modern or open-minded. It is politics down below. Marriage translates into citizens with their primary allegiance to the family. Free love creates spinning souls available to the State. Capitalism vs Communism, think about it!

The Friend

Now don't tell me you have never seen a human writhe with envy? Of anything and anyone with the remotest shine on them. A promotion takes place few degrees from them, and they dip the first spoon into their heart. A beautiful wedding comes together in the neighbourhood, and their blood changes colour. Someone fortunate shares their child's accomplishment in their hearing, and our friend begins to pant. This species shares certain characteristics. It foams a bit at the mouth. The eyes dart across a room full of people, assessing their social dynamics. Beware of the innocent sounding "What's up?" Your yakkety yak is the fuel that will drive this jealous jalopy. Watch them dish the dirt to their newest victim at gatherings. There is always this "us vs the world" theme to these whispering willows. "Have you heard? Come here, I have something to tell you? So and so is plotting your downfall?!" The sucker teehees gamely, beginning to warm up to the tap of acid. It is human, this sharp thrill at being pulled aside by an oblique face. You feel you are the chosen one. You think the tattler is tearing your contemporary world in a team spirit with you. You think this badmouth is your buddy for life. Come September and watch the turncoats get their foot up on your lumbar and graduate to the next quarry while you flail in the jettison. Be prepared to watch the grand new partnership from a distance, debating whether to forewarn the buyer. But you are too nice. You are above the sniping. You have better things to do than to call out a mischief maker's bluff. And well, nobody warned you! If they did, you felt secure in the knowledge that you are different and the compost carry-on is actually quite good at heart. It is not in our culture, moreover, to bell the cats.

The Banal

Do know, dear woman, that this one human emotion is the moral property of men? You are permitted the pressure cooker but not the whistle. It is apparently the ugliest sight in the world: a woman radiating an honest to goodness fury. The petulant pout is acceptable. The measured stamping of toes will also do; remember to twist a piece of cloth and bat the eyelids and wag the neck. But heaven help you if you dare glare at the world with a white-hot rage at an imagined injustice. Your job is to keep peace and construct male entitlement. And you get to be a spoilt princess, a hormonal teen, a high-maintenance wife, or a shrill nag. What more would you need? Just keep your feelings to yourself and work around male needs, no! Did you not know that the signal emotion of anger has been assigned a gender? A basic human sentiment that is neither good nor bad but useful to warn of indignity, insult, or threat has been appropriated by men. He owns road rage, impatience, and second guessing; for you, dear lady, God has ordained deference. Cross your legs, tame that hair, and remember to bite your tongue as you are swallowing your pride. You don't want to risk being called rude and unlikable. Let your body thrum with silent and isolating fury instead; it will leach into your organs and settle in as chronic pain. Cry into your pillow, mutter under your breath, kick and punch out of their sight, but maintain the appearance of an admiring, available, and appreciative passenger. Men brought up in the glow of unfiltered adulation from mothers and sisters will only be angry at your anger. They are unlikely to ask a hissing harpy in a gentle tone, "What is bothering you woman? Can I help?" The world's quota is only one Goddess Durga. And it's ok. You don't have to take yourself so seriously.

The Coupon

Have you spent four times the value of a discount coupon just so it wouldn't die out on you? Has anyone done the maths? Is it a profitable deal in the final analysis? You tuck the perforated ribbon of delusions into your bag with a surge of smug energy, like the cat with the milk. There is a benign warmth in the heart. You have currency that you can call in at will. It feels good. The first trip you make to redeem the coupon, you amble around the store like a king, heat radiating from the pocket. Ah, that smart, hand-painted tray set of three, so very elegant in cobalt. You congratulate yourself at the find and fetch up at the checkout counter, pretending nonchalance at the treat awaiting you. Just as you pull out your wallet, the clerk flicks your precious ticket back at you. "It's for clothes. Apparel only!" You want to lift him by the scruff and flutter your epiglottis in his face, but there are fidgety folks behind you, and you are feeling foolish and fooled. Who reads the fine print in this country anyway? We trust the systems historically. A week of recovery, and you are back to fretting at the calendar; the expiration is at approaching fast now. The horror of impending loss nags at your heart. You are too Indian to pass up an economic concession. Your soul is so stirred at the vanishing value; you marshal the family for a trip to the store in the festive of all the seasons. In the war zone of discount sales, you are seized with the famine syndrome. The shopping cart fills up rapidly. The sales trick has worked. The business snared you in, sold you several more products at full price, and made you feel smart. There's a term for it: operating profit.

183

The Mandate

Are you that child who cost her parent the least to bring up? It used to be such a virtue held up to the siblings and the rest of the extended family as a glittering example. You were a good kid if you did not tax your parents too much. Such simple times, having children lionized for saving you expense. There is another synonym for it today. It is called an inability to occupy space. A failure to have your needs met. A lack of social assertiveness. The mantra is self-care, and it's not because the new generations are selfish. They happen to be growing up in harsher times. The bared envy, the pressure to succeed, the impossible celebrity looks to live up to, the emotional mayhem, the debilitating social media, a malevolent press, and mentally ill political leaders. No wonder our young see through all the bullshit. Better not use condescension or patronage in your communications with this deep, intelligent, and empathic progeny. They know you for the self-seeking hypocrite you are. Talk straight with sincerity and honesty around them. They are suffering a brand of existential angst you and I wouldn't know if it hit us in our third eyes. Of course, you tie yourself up in knots asking, "My goodness, they have everything: great education, good looks, ultra-supportive parents, crowing grandparents. What more could they want? Why don't they just snap out of it? They have too much time. They don't exercise enough!" Careful. Careful. There is a dark sadness many of them are suspended in. It's hard to tell from the FB or Instagram or Tumblr posts what their struggles with self-worth and life's meaning are. Paradoxically, our anthem to raise independent children has resulted in a crop that needs us more and longer and in a variety of avatars than any gone before. Ears, compass, confidante, cheerleader, ally, punching bag…throw all the judgement, fear, and ego out the front door. Strap up and sit back. These are unique young lives at stake, and we have miles to go. No saying about the sleep!

The Lights

Have you sat in your car, heart in the mouth, idling at a red light counting down from seventy-seven? You are primed for disaster to strike. Muscles rippling in copious adrenaline, you recite the Gayatri Mantra, peering into the rear-view mirror for approaching canons. It is unprecedented, your traffic conduct. Your countrymen don't expect vehicles to halt at traffic signals at six am when the roads are whistle clean. It is sixty seconds now in the aerial clock. You narrow your eyes at a jaywalker stealing up from the right. He is tentative! He takes a step forward, then two back, swinging on the balls, measuring you up for intent. *Who, in his right mind, stops at signals on deserted roads?* you watch him think. You feel torn. You want to hide in shame but reassure him your foot is off the throttle. He darts across all of a sudden, death wish written all over his nebulous face. Phew! Forty-five seconds to go. A scooter grumbles by brashly. You look ahead, a study in stone face. Let him think you are a museum piece. Ah, two pools of low beam edge up on the right. You straighten up. See, there is a legitimacy in your decision to waste fuel and time. Next, you raise your eyes and scan the treetops like a fox. Where are the cameras? Is Google Earth upon your sneaky core yet? The blue lines flicker down to fifteen. Your right toe tips towards the gas pedal, left raised ever so slightly. Oh, hells bells, a hissing metal monster is taking shape from the haze behind. It's an SUV exuding testosterone. The cartilage in your ears crack at the strains of "High rated Gabru." This is a determined Delhite! Your life begins to zip past the eyes. Your reflexes take over. The count is nine. You launch! The faithful Honda ricochets past the divider to career towards the trees up ahead. You play the power steering frantically, shrinking back from the blustery blue Kia Seltos. Crunch. You hear the metal fold up. And the green flicks on!

185

The Step

Have you been in a close hold with a stranger during a social dance class? It is a study in comic relief. Oh, you keep the hands light, fighting shy of leaving an impression on his shirt. In fact, two kinds of partners are at a tremendous advantage: the giants and the dwarfs. Neither need wrestle with the frightening eye level! You are either making faces at his mid torso, or he is peering at your crown hair wave in the wake of his breath. The problem is with physically-compatible partners who have to twirl and spin while keeping their eyes carefully averted. The instructor suggests helpfully that everyone look at their partner and not at their toes. But not a hair turns on any ear, and class remains rigidly polite by counting under their breath or laser-beaming the pair in their neighbourhood. What to do? You know how we *desis* are? The generations up until now, in particular. We are not all that touchy feely; there hasn't been the space or the time or the emotional permission from family to practice the human touch. We have culturally connected with the other's epidermis either for a blessing or to land a blow. Of course, we experience intimacy in our country within the four walls, but in most cases, the nature of connection is extremely localized and directed at asserting conjugal rights or adding to the family. Catch anyone wasting time on dead end embraces or just good old affection. As the class progresses and everyone gets a handle on the steps, the masks begin to slip. And they come off altogether when a married couple comes face to face during the partner change drill. The disconnect flashes like a red siren, and you glimpse the modern muddle that is marriage today. He clearly is a step behind. Literally.

The Exchange

Have you received an invite that entreated you not to carry a gift, please? You narrow your eyes at the text and bite your lip, gauging its seriousness. The hostess's face flashes in your visual cortex. You try to visualize her visage in the two situations: as a beneficiary and a non-beneficiary. Neither of the images give you any courage. How does one tell if they are just being polite? What if the other guests come bearing voluminous offerings! And horror of horrors, should everyone decide to toe the line. You have been wanting, moreover, to get rid of that particular lamp in your gift inventory for six months now; this event seemed perfectly placed in terms of hierarchy and exchange history, but now this exhortation. You take the dilemma to the lord and master. "Don't overthink. They don't want anything. Period," he pronounces. But your brain is in gear by now. Sometime, during the day, you throw open your coffer and stare at the contents. There is a cookie cutter set you picked up five years ago from a store in Chicago. Ah, those two books! Darn, they are addressed to you on the title page. How about that useless panel of patchwork? It has been awaiting its turn for aeons. You bang the social survival kit shut, drawing a deep breath, having arrived at the decision to obey. But as the day approaches, your courage begins to wane. Perhaps some flowers or maybe a bag of boutique cookies. Wine! Nobody counts it a gift anymore! It is just an accessory you carry to an event, knowing fully well it will find use again. As an accessory. It doesn't occur to you to put any other thought into it. What are your host's interests? What would simply make them quiver with delight? A day before the party, you give in and select a listless piece from your aged hoard, wrapping it in an inelegant rush. It ends up being a feel-bad exercise you would rather not dwell upon. On your way out of their festive home, you are recounting reading about the South American spider that woos his mate with prey wrapped in silk, including low quality prey or just the remains of one he has already consumed. No prizes for guessing what the creepy crawly busies himself with while his lady is unwrapping the gift. But then gifting is connecting. It is the defining and strengthening of our life bonds. Done thoughtfully, both the giver and the taker stand to receive an equal amount of pleasure.

The Door

Have you struggled with a closed door in your house ever? No, it's not jammed. It has been deliberately and firmly shut and latched with an intention to keep you out. Go ahead. Knock. First gently, then insistently, and soon with an ear flattened against the wood. Call tentatively to begin with, then louder, but the music is insurmountable. Your innards begin to erupt now. Some guests are expected home, and you want to forewarn the kid. Perhaps you want the curtains inside measured for a makeover. Quite likely, it's the family dog you think has gotten locked in. Even a fire, God forbid! But the door stays in place. You stand rooted for one paralyzed moment, then shuffle away in bewilderment. Oh, good lord, what if he is writhing in fever! Hope he has not passed out, horizontal in an alcoholic haze. You bolt back at the door. There's a gap between the panels. You grab the handles and apply pressure, sinking to an arthritic haunch. While you are craning to align the eye, the domestic happens upon his crouching madam. "Dukhi, I dropped the tiny screw on my ear stud; use your broom later alright!" You heave up, exhaling an exasperated sigh while he looks on, squinting at you limping off in a cloud of injured dignity. But the needles of suspicion are stabbing at you. Betoo's toe had just begun to come into view when you were interrupted. What if he suffered a stroke having smoked up until dawn with his scruffy bros. Could he have been poring over porn? Beads of sweat threaten your forehead now. You reach for your loyal bottle of Sualin and pop a tablet, wincing at the sickly sweetness. Lowering gingerly on to the edge of your bed, you address yourself, "Try looking in from the windows across his room. Get up!" Just as you are picking yourself, a dispirited young voice comes cutting through the corridor, "Ma, I sent you a WhatsApp message last night to wake me up at 6 am; I just missed an important session. Don't you guys check your feeds?"

The Moves

What is that one arena in India where it is perfectly legitimate to be lascivious and come hither? A trifle cheap as they say. Fleshy, undulating, and mock seductive. You can throw your head back, tip it one way, or even cock it. The eyes could be dilated under twitching brows, narrowed for coquettish effect, or just plain rolled and crossed playfully. No one bats an eyelid! Looking in from the outside, it would appear to be a rally called "Humans against inhibitions." It's alright, you can use your handkerchief as a prop. Just bite one corner and pinch the other with both hands. Now swing the head, both arms, and the waist to mimic coil uncoil. Don't worry about your appearance. There is sure to be a human snake close by, hands cupped over his expressive head, lunging at thin air. You don't have a buoy, simply imagine one. A stack of currency notes for one. Careful now, this needs skill. You begin to flick them into the sky with the right index finger and off the left palm, gyrating all the time. Bend those knees a bit. Such a suicidal but celebratory sense of abandon, quite un-Indian. It is perfectly acceptable to balance a full glass of the amber beverage on head and teeter, egged on by bashful beams on glistening faces. This is the safe space for the most part to let the hair down. You are free to cut the rug in multiple directions. Be as jerky, as twirly, as trippy as you like; you know perfectly well that just beyond the floor lies your true, dignified self. This is just pretend. A hark back to our Bollywood subconscious. A glimpse of the play that lurks in the heart. A window to the primal masquerade. And you are in plenty company even as you pirouette around a bellowing dupatta. The spectators! Their mirror neurons are lit and frisky.

The Bargain

Have you nursed a stormy relationship with our cultural talent for bargaining? You are either proud of your ability to haggle or filled with annoyance at another's mastery. It is almost a national sport to pour cold water on anyone springing their hard-earned purchase by bringing out a rival, cheaper one. The technique is to rub salt into the injured wounds by sharing where they could have gotten it for way lesser. We, therefore, live with a perpetual disquiet; there is little pleasure in spending our money, courtesy the fear that somewhere someone smarter has pulled off a better deal. It would still be bearable if the friend gloated less. But so superior is this virtue deemed that they have to lick their chops in your clouding eyes. It is relentless, this pursuit of a bargain; it takes us flocking to the brand sales and offers and exchanges. And no, the expertise has not needed any training yet. Having been a nation that has been invaded more than two hundred times, our victim mentality is sharp as a tack. It is in our DNA to whine, cajole, and blackmail the seller. Bargaining is to India what programming is to the Silicon Valley. The threat now is from the once deluxe economies. Our former masters have taken to haggling for one, stiff upper lip and all. The Yankees have already patented turmeric as a healing agent and basmati as their long-grained rice. The art and science of bargaining is traditional knowledge we cannot afford to have usurped by another people.

190
The Penalty

Have you pulled into a parking spot with a sigh of relief only to have the bumptious attendant descend upon you in a cacophony of whistles? He is waiting in the wings, watching you wiggle into the tricky spot. Just as you let go of your straining muscles and flop back dead, he shows up at your window, "Sirji, please pull out and park it a bit closer to this white car here." You want to vaporize him with molten eyes. You want to sob with fatigue. You want to implore him to let you be. But he is both dismissive and insistent. You seethe and snort, waving at the cavalier manner several others have parked their vehicles in. "You! You! You there, where the hell were you cosying up when I rolled in? Just look at you sauntering in while I fall behind my appointment. You cause me to waste precious fuel, 74.05 per litre!" There is a sign up, moreover, warning owners that they park at their own risk. "This nation will never change," you sputter to yourself. An uncivilized, self-seeking lot of humbugs, the countrymen. You congratulate the government for levying the heavy traffic fines. There does, after all, need to be deterrence. Your colleagues at the meeting echo your opinions when you join them in a cloud of profuse apologies. With business done, you head back home now; a friend riding shotgun. So absorbed are you both with all that the nation needs to know, you breeze through an amber light. The Marshall looms into view from the epileptic traffic. "Your licence will be confiscated, and you will have to recover it after paying 5000 rupees online." Your righteous halo vanishes under the weight of this unexpected expenditure. Your friend scrambles up to your ear. An urgent whisper, and it is settled at 500 rupees. "Go," the state representative says, his voice greasy. You drive home, fighting stabs of ignominy. "At least I don't keep both odd and even number plates at home," you soothe yourself.

191

The Prude

Have you driven past a movie hall, stealing surreptitious glances at the bold billboard? "Gupt gyan," it declares, almost like a dare. You must have been one short of your teen years back then. There was this hush-hush air about the movie. Those were erotically challenged times in retrospect. A lot under the carpet, more behind open umbrellas, and the rest within the four walls. Hearts stayed where they belonged, in the thoracic cavity. Godfather, Lolita, and the odd Playboy magazine comprised the entire spectrum of sex education for the baby boomers. Mandakini in *Ram Teri Ganga Maili* and Zeenat Aman in *Satyam Shivam Sundaram* would have seared many a triggered mind. Reams were written on the bold scenes of Rehana Sultan in films like *Chetna* and *Dastak*. And who can forget Lakshmi as the lush Julie against Vikram as the fervid Shashi Bhattacharya. Then comes Bobby in her ascendant dress and dewdrop face. Those were the "Gapoochi Gapoochi Gam Gam" days. So much was *Khel Khel Mein*. It took a simple finger on a fainting woman's pulse to confirm pregnancy. Shame shrouded both private and public life, much like New Delhi's asphyxiating pollution. The unutterably gruesome word people only hissed in asides to describe a relationship was "affair." You could never be in one; you had to have had 'had' an affair. And it was red in colour! Boys and girls in co-ed schools were the fifth and sixth castes. They barely spoke to each other. The only acceptable social connection between the two genders was that of siblings. You were either brother and sister or husband and wife. Mainstream genders were only two in number. Who would have known the pleasure fest waiting to break upon the subcontinent? And with such an array of arrangements. You could hang out, hook up, or be into. You could be bread-crumbing, peacocking, or micro-cheating. You could be in a relationship or a talkship or a situationship. Mono, bi, or poly? Decision paralysis or a healthy compromise? Just like a cereal shopper in the Big Bazaar!

Epilogue

At her NLSIU (National Law School of India University) memorial hosted by her batchmates, we heard the following: (paraphrasing)

* Aqs taught us to speak our truth without fear of disapproval

* She had no time to bitch about anyone

* Aqs was woke, way before her time

* Such a beautiful dancer

* She found the subalterns wherever she went and gave them strength

* Aqs never had a plan B

Aqseer has gone and we are left listening to this song by Don McLean-Vincent (Starry, Starry Night), the words are so apt:

Now, I understand what you tried to say to me

And how you suffered for your sanity

And how you tried to set them free

They would not listen, they did not know how

Perhaps they'll listen now

For they could not love you

But still your love was true

And when no hope was left inside

On that starry, starry night

You took your life as lovers often do

But I could have told you, Vincent

This world was never meant for one

As beautiful as you

The other thing we do is plant the Bleeding-Heart vine (Clerodendrum thomsoniae) in our homes and those of our friends to honour the biggest Bleeding heart of them all: Aqseer Sodhi.

Other Generational Books by Author